"A Steward and Superintendent of Many Years Practice"

Practical Treatise on the Nature of Brewing

Threale, Thomas

The Complete Family-Brewer

Watkins, George

The Compleat English Brewer

Crocker, Abraham

The Art of Making and Managing Cyder

ISBN: 978-1-948837-03-3

This classic reprint compilation was produced from digital files in the Google Books digital collection, which may be found at http://www.books.google.com. The artwork used on the cover is from Wikimedia Commons and remains in the public domain. Omissions and/or errors in this book are due to either the physical condition of the original book or due to the scanning process by Google or its agents.

Practical Treatise on the Nature of Brewing was originally published in 1801 (London); Thomas Threale's **The Complete Family-Brewer** was originally published in 1802 (London); George Watkins's **The Compleat English Brewer** was originally published in 1768 (London); and Abraham Crocker's **The Art of Making and Managing Cyder** was originally published in 1806 (Tauton).

Townsends
PO Box 415, Pierceton, IN 46562
www.Townsends.us

TABLE OF CONTENTS

Section One

Section Two

CONTENTS

CONTENTS

CONTENTS

Section Four

The Butlers & Publicans Assistant on BREWING, &c. &c. &c.

PRACTICAL TREATISE

ON THE NATURE OF

BREWING

Fine, Wholesome, Brilliant, and Rich High-Flavoured

WELCH & SCURVY-GRASS ALES,

AND

Strong Beers,

With London Porter and Brown Stout,

Fine TABLE BEER, &c.

AND

THE MANAGEMENT OF WINES, CHEESE, CELLARS, &c. &c.

BY

A Steward & Superintendant,

OF MANY YEARS PRACTICE.

THE SECOND EDITION, WITH MANY IMPROVEMENTS.

PRINTED FOR THE AUTHOR,

BY W. SMITH, NO. 49, KING STREET, SEVEN DIALS;

And ſold by Barratt, at Bath; Branſby, Ipſwich; Thompſon, Mancheſter; Richardſon, Bate and Son, Royal Exchange; Murray and Highley, Fleet Street; R. B. Scott, 378, Strand; Sutton, Long Acre, near St. Martin's Lane; E. Harding, Pall Mall; Laking, Curzon Street, May Fair; Hookham, Old Bond Street; Archer, Dublin; and by the principal Bookſellers in England and Ireland.

1801.

Price Two Shillings.

TO THE PUBLIC.

THE Author of this ſmall treatiſe has always thought it a moſt eſſential point, that families who live in the country (and especially those who are large, and ſee a deal of company) ſhould be very curious and particular in having good, ſound, and wholeſome malt liquors, *as nothing can be so great a credit to them, or so* cheap and wholeſome a beverage; *and from being a witneſs to ſo much neglect on that head, either through ignorance or inattention (or perhaps both) has induced him to write a plain and eaſy guide upon* BREWING, *from many years experience; which if properly attended to, no one* can err, *for it is within the* reach of every capacity—*and from the reception it has met with by* FAMILIES OF THE FIRST DISTINCTION, *merits his moſt grateful acknowledgments.*

Note—*The great demand for the above Treatise, since its first publication, is the best proof of its* real merits; *indeed no* Family, Butler, *or* Publican, *ſhould be without one.*

PRACTICAL TREATISE.

THE day before the brewing is intended, let the copper be heated, in order to *cleanse it,* with the *caſks, maſh-tub, coolers, &c.* Then fill your copper, and put every thing in readineſs for next morning, and the malt in the maſh-tub, except about half a buſhel; obſerving to place the baſket before the cock-hole on the inſide, with a clean wiſp of ſtraw, to prevent the malt coming into the cock.

As ſoon as the copper boils, put on the quantity of water you intend to make upon the malt, (allowing four pails for the grains to ſuck up,) and as the boiling water is lading on the malt, let it be kept well ſtirred up; and then run the big end of the maſh-oar through the middle of it, and there let it ſtand, taking the ſpare half-buſhel of malt to cover the other over with; then cover the tub over with ſacks to keep the ſteam in, and *let it remain ſo two hours.*

It is proper you ſhould know what the *copper holds*; and indeed it ought to hold full ſeventy gallons, becauſe the hogſhead is ſixty-three gallons, and what of the hops, and the ſufficient room it ſhould have for working them about when it boils, to *procure their eſſence*, and prevent waſte. If the copper is not of that ſize, it had better be changed for one of that dimenſion, and the bottom to be made ſtout; then you need only boil four times for the *ſtrong* and *table beer*, or *ale* and *table beer*: for if the copper is ſmaller, you muſt do it oftener, which is a great *waſte of coals* as well as time. But if the family is large, the copper had better hold twice ſeventy gallons, for then you can brew either two hogſheads of *ſtrong beer*, or two of *ale* at a time, and the ſame quantity of table beer. If your employer would wiſh to have all his *caſks good*, and of one ſize, (which is certainly preferable,) nothing can be more durable than the iron-bound rum puncheons, for they hold in general one hundred and twenty gallons, which will be near two hogſheads of beer meaſure; they may be purchaſed from 12s. to 14s. each, and with care will laſt years.

Pay great attention to the copper, for the moment it is emptied it muſt be filled; and if at any time it boils too faſt, open the door, and fling in ſome *ſlack* (that is, *wet ſmall coal or cinders*,) which ſhould always be uſed to brew with, reſerving the round coals for the parlours, &c. for *economy* ſhould be obſerved at all times.

By the time the copper boils for the *table beer* (and that will be about an hour) then let the cock be half turned, to run upon the hops that are intended to be uſed, into a tub under the cock for that purpoſe, *rubbing the hops between the hands till all are wet*:

but before the tub goes under the cock, draw a pail-full firſt, as it will cauſe it to *run finer*; and when all is run off the malt into the tub of hops, let the water be immediately put on the malt for the table beer, keeping it maſhed as before, and put the pail of ſtrong beer to the ſmall. When all is on, cover it with the bags, the ſame as the other, the maſh oar ſtanding in the middle of it; *and this muſt be two hours likewiſe.*

While this is doing, the ſtrong beer and hops is put into the copper, and there kept gently boiling for *two hours*, ſtirring it all the time; after the two hours are expired, the hair ſieve is placed upon the cooler to ſtrain the hops through, and when the ſieve is full, it is brought down into the tub below the maſh-tub, and the table beer ſet running on them in the ſame manner as the ſtrong beer. When the copper is empty, then get up the table beer into it, and boil it *two hours, the ſame as the ſtrong*; and when ſo done, ſtrain it into the other coolers, reſerving half a pailful of the hops for the purpoſe I ſhall ſpeak of hereafter.

You ſee by this time how the ſtrong and table beer is *brewed*, (that is to ſay) each is to ſtand on the malt two hours, and each to boil two hours, that is *eight hours; and I defy any man to have ſour or bad beer in his cellars*, if managed in this manner, and a proper quantity of malt and hops are allowed: and ſurely it is to every *nobleman and gentleman's intereſt to allow them*, for bad weak beer is not only *unwholeſome*, but half is waſted and thrown away; while the *good* will not ſtand any gentleman in more than four-pence half-penny a quart, *beſides having the fine table beer gratis, which will always be a credit to him and his table*—and then when his cellars are well ſtocked, what a ſupport to his family, and infinite pleaſure in knowing that in thoſe *beers* there is nothing but pure *malt, water and hops.*

The allowance of malt for *strong beer* must be *ten bussels to the hogshead,* and for ale *nine;* then there will come a good hogshead of table beer from each: and there must be a *pound of hops* for every bushel of malt. —This will make the nalt liquors *high-flavored and good.*

As the copper is now heating to cleanſe it, and the tubs ready to receive the ſtrong and table beer out of the coolers, &c. when ſo cleaned, the people muſt be informed what time to come for the grains out of the way; for the moment each of the beers are as *cool as milk from the cow,* the tubs are put under the coolers, for the beer to run into; then, with a quart of fine yeaſt to each, ſtir it well about with a wooden bowl, (one for the ſtrong and another for the table beer,) and turn them up topſy-turvy in the middle of each tub, which occaſions the beer to work; but if you find, in about two hours, that it does not work kind, put the maſh-oar, &c. a-croſs the tubs, and cover them with ſacks; and the laſt thing before you go to bed, and the firſt thing in the morning, ſtir them both well up again; but be careful your tubs are *not too full to work over in the night.*

The next day, which is the second morning, ſkim the greateſt part of the yeaſt off, and prepare to tun it. Let the caſks be taken *quite clean and warm into the cellars,* firſt examining the cock and vent-holes; and when filled, you will have ſome ſpare beer of each, as it works, ready at hand, to fill them up with in the cellars; but as ſoon as full, take 2 lb. of fine flour, and beat it up ſmooth with ſome of the new beer, with a whiſp, and equally divide it between the two barrels, keeping it well ſtirred for a quarter of an hour; and in all beer and ale you brew do not forget the flour, and equally divide it into each caſk, letting it be well ſtirred up for five minutes; then put the tin ſcoop into the upper cock-hole for it to work through, *and attend it every two or three hours; particularly the laſt thing at night and firſt in the morning;* and when done working, which is generally in three days, let the outſides of the barrels be well cleaned, and the hops ſaved in the pail divided into each, and then *bung them tight down; putting the date on them when brewed.* If your family admire fine *Welch ales* for the ſummer months, in lieu of boiling the wort two hours, let it only boil an hour, but as faſt as you can make it boil; and have ready to fling in the copper twelve pound of brown moiſt ſugar, keeping it well ſtirred up the whole time, and particularly from the bottom; and as it is not brewed for beer to keep, half a pound of hops to every buſhel will be ſufficient; and before you want to tap it (which may be done in three or four months) fine it as I have already deſcribed, and you will find it of that *ſoft, rich, fine flavour that Welch ales in general poſſeſs.* I have fre-

C

quently brewed it the beginning of March, and in June following found it *moſt excellent.*

While all this is doing, you are preparing for brewing again, in filling the copper, &c. for no time muſt be loſt during the cool months; eſpecially if the family is large.

As moſt *Noblemen and Gentlemen take great pride to outvie each other in having ſuperior articles about their tables, &c. than their neighbours,* you cannot be *too curious in malt liquors, &c.* under your management; I ſhall therefore adviſe you, ten days before you want either *ſtrong or table beer for the uſe of the parlour,* to peg a caſk of each, in order to take them of the *beſt quality and flavour* (for what is ſurpriſing every caſk will differ); and when ſo done, and you have made your choice, put a good handful of the ſhavings of iſinglaſs into a ſtewpan three parts filled with the ſame ſtrong beer intended to be tapped, and let it ſimmer gently over a ſlow fire for an hour, then pour it into a pail, and draw the pail three parts full, and equally divide it between the ſtrong and ſmall beer, ſtirring it well up with a long ſtick for a quarter of an hour, and then bung it tight down an hour afterwards; and two days before you want it, let it be tapped, and draw off a *quart or two of each,* for this will help *to fine it greatly*; and always make uſe of ſtrainer cocks, and keep the vent-pegs tight in, with a tap-tub under each cock: *this beer* will be of great repute in your family, and it will be admired by every viſitor likewiſe, for nothing will be more *brilliant and tranſparent,* or *finer beverage,* with cheeſe, &c. but at any time you find it begins to be ſtale for the parlour uſe, tap two others in the ſame manner, and uſe the ſtale for the family, drawing a little of the new to it.

If you wiſh to brew fine *Scurvy-Graſs Ales* (which no doubt is fine for the Spring Seaſon by the ſame mode you brew the Welch ales, you will brew the *Scurvy-Graſs Ale*; and when your copper boils with the wort, have ready to throw into it half a buſhel of fine wormwood, and 12 lb. of ſugar, that is to ſay, if you brew a hogſhead; but if only a 36 gallon barrel, half that quantity; and as it will be drank in the ſpring, it needs no hops.

Again, as no man can be a *good butler*, &c. unleſs he takes delight in his *cellars*; and to be a good *cellarman and good brewer*, attention muſt be paid to *cleanlineſs, &c. which is a very requiſite qualification*; and every man intruſted with the *care of cellars*, and the management of liquors, &c. &c. ought to pride himſelf in having them *clean*, and every thing in *order*, as much as the *dining parlour and drawing room*. You will, therefore, during the ſummer months have the beer-cellar waſhed out weekly, and the tap tubs every other day; it is not only pleaſant, but keeps the beer *fine and cool*, and if neglected, it will cauſe the beer to turn ſour; and in the winter months, ſweeping them out once a week will be ſufficient; and make a memorandum from this paper, of all things you ſtand in need of, ſhewing the liſt to your *employer*. A large cock for the maſh-tub will be found more preferable than a ſpicket and fauſcet, which often flies out, and is a great waſte.

The following are the Neceſſaries always wanted for the Cellars, viz.

Shot, and lead caniſter, and two cloths to waſh bottles (and beware of any bottles that has had oil in) may be kept in the bottle rack

Two large tubs to be kept for that purpoſe only

Six ſtrain cocks, bungs, corks, vent-pegs, and mallet

A pair of pliers, and cork-drawer

A leather boot to buckle on the knee, to hold the bottles in when corking them

A ſtrong mahogany cork driver

Coarſe linen to put under the bungs

Six tin ſpouts, made as broad as a banker's ſhovel, for the beer to work through

A ſtrong iron ſkewer to raiſe the bungs up with

A middle-ſized gimblet

A quire of ſtout brown paper to put round cocks

Two large ſponges, to clean the out-ſides of the caſks, &c. with

Two ſplit broom-ſticks, for cellar candleſticks

Six iron-bound tap tubs

A wine bitt, to bore the caſks with

Two long wine cocks

A bruſh for to bruſh the mites off the cheeſe

A flogger to beat up the wine bungs, with

Two pails

13

Two tin funnels, to put in spare bottles when bottling off
Two low stools to sit on
A lether apron, with a pocket before, and bib to button up on the waistcoat
A flannel bag, made the same as a jelly bag, to run lees through
A common cork screw
An iron bound wine can, for fining wines in
A hoe, spade, and six good stiff birch brooms
And, above all, good and sufficient locks and keys upon all the cellar doors

The use of the iron skewer is to raise up the bungs by degrees, first giving it vent with the skewer, for drawing it up with hands is very dangerous.

Have a strong flat basket made to hold all the tools in, and put the basket with them on one of the barrels, so that you have everything thing at hand when wanted; and if the cellars are dark, have a lamp of common oil burning, for drawing beer in the dark will cause waste.

In choosing the malt, take especial care that it is not peat or straw dried; and do not have it too pale a colour, or to ohigh, but in the medium; and every Gentleman that studies his own interest, would do well to buy the malt unground, for there he would have the fine flower and quintessence of it, which will abundantly repay for a malt mill and grinding; and whether he adopts this method or not, it is always requisite to have the mail maeasured, as it is putting into the mash-tub, and the hops weighed, for care and exactness should be attended to.

The best hops are certainly the Kentish.

The choice months are March and October to brew in.

If the casts should prove musty at any time, have the cooper to unhead them, and burn them out; and see what hoops, &c. are wanting to the others; but the moment a cask becomes empty, stop up the bung and cock hole tight, which will be a means to keep them always sweet; and when all is put in good condition, a cooper will seldom be required.

As you cannot be to ocareful of things put under your charge, have a double padlock and key to screw on the brewhouse door, (particularly when any malt or beer is about) recollecting that part of scripture, "Well done thou good and faithful servant, thou hast been faithful over a few things; I will make thee ruler over many." But place yourself frequently in your master's situation, and then judge what you would expect from him, if he were in your's. This will instantly convince you that you are never to waste your master's time or property; and that you should be conscientiously careful of little things; that you should never (like an eye servant) take advantage of your master's absence; that it would be wrong to listen to private conversation, or to look into private papers, and very wrong indeed to report the secrets or weaknesses of the family:

keeping in view the importance of maintaining a *good character*; and never be fond of changing your situation; and once for all, "A still tongue *makes a wise head*."

Be careful that no soap or grease comes about the tubs or pails, *that will prevent the beer from working*; and never suffer them to be used for any other purpose; and mind your liquor-stands are very steady, and not to rock.

Note—Observe never to *bottle* in the cellar *wine, beer, or cyder*, but of a *fine clear day*, and *let the bottles be well inspected*; and use no corks *but the velvet ones*.

As *porter* may be approved of (from being a great novelty in the country) and as you know how to brew good sound strong *beers*, I need not take up much of your time to inform you how to brew good *London porter* in the country. The world would not believe till lately, that *porter* could be brewed at any other place than London, on account of the *Thames water*; when, for instance, the first brewer in the kingdom * uses no other than the New River water; and it is well known now that porter is brewed in most of the principal towns in England, Ireland, &c. &c. and therefore if a man can brew good beer and ale, he can brew good porter, for it is all done by the same *process*, only to *observe* the malt must be a *brown malt*, in lieu of the other you use for ale and strong beer; and the hops a full *fine brown hop*; and then when your

* Samuel Whitbread, Esq.

wort and hops are boiling, have ready to put into the copper (for every hogshead you intend to brew) three pound of bruised liquorice root, cut short, three quarters of a pound of Spanish liquorice, and eight pound of coarse brown moist sugar; and let it gently boil for two hours as beforesaid, keeping it well stirred up from the bottom, &c. the whole time; and then strain the hops off, and put it into your coolers the same as the other beers, and in six months it will be fit for use; and as you want no table beer from this, eight bushel of malt, and eight pound of hops will do. The sugar is an agreeable sweet and a fine bitter, and greatly adds to the strngth of the porter.

As fine bottle table beer *is esteemed by most families during the ſummer months,* always have ſome bottled off; the old corks will do for this uſe.

If you want to brew what is called *Brown Stout Porter,* allow nine buſhels and a half to the hogſhead, and as many pound of hops, and I will warrant it to *resist any climate*; and if any is exported, never let it be racked off, but ſent in the ſame caſk, as it is tunned in; for all beer *lives and feeds upon its grounds and hops,* and inſtead of being flat when it arrives, will be briſk and fine; and in lieu of vent pegs, you muſt get from the ironmongers *vent nails,* for they ſhift up and down themſelves; as the beer requires; and if you bottle any porter to uſe at home, or ſend abroad, let it be the *brown stout*; for with *oysters, cheeſe,* &c. it is *delicious*; and let it be ſix months old before you bottle it; but if you bottle any to go *abroad*, let it be drawed in the bottles forty-eight hours to flatten it, before it is corked, and then wire them with brafs wire, cut for that purpofe into lengths, and pack them in *cafks*, round and round; and after every fecond layer is in, get into the cafk with your fhoes on, and jump your whole weight upon them, for they muft be preffed as tight in the old dry ftraw packing as *bricks in a wall*; and when your cafks are full, let the cooper head them.

Porter, after a voyage, is a hundred per cent. before any drank that has never been on the feas.

After the porter is fined in the manner the other beer is, to make it have a fine head lower your hand a diftance from the cock, and let it run down the fide, to make it froth, leaving lip room on the top of the pot.

If you want to fine a pipe of wine, the fhells and whites of twenty frefh new-laid eggs, beat up ten minutes with a whifp, mixed with about two quarts of the wine, is a moft excellent fining for all wines, and nothing *pernicious*; this is to be flung into the cafk, and ftirred well up with a long ftick for about a quarter of an hour, and in about half an hour afterwards, put the bung down tight: but never attempt to peg wine, or any other liquor, to fee if it is fine, *but of a fine clear day*, for the foul air will certainly get in; and before you bottle it off, let your bottles be *well infpected*, and taken down in prickles ready.

E

18

Beer and cyder must stand in bottles six hours before they are corked; the latter should be wired and packed in a bin with sand, and the former in a dry deal saw-dust.

As this book will fall into the hands of many publicans, especially those in the country, they will do well first to consider before they brew, what they will sell their beer for; and then reckon their malt, hops, fire, labour and duty; which will enable them to judge what quantity of malt they ought to allow for each hogshead, to live by their trade. One thing they may depend upon, and that is, when their beer is fine and bright, and of a good flavour, they may always charge a penny a quart extra; and by saving it so, they make their houses known and respected. the same mode may be observed in porter and scurvy-grass ale of their own brewing.

The wine cellars should have good, double, inside inclosed doors, to fit close, to prevent air, &c. coming in them, which would save the expence and unwholesome effect of charcoal in the winter, in a brazier, &c.

Note—be careful of your empty bottles; there should be a sufficient bottle rack to hold them, with folding doors, and a good double padlock and key to lock them up; and when there is two or three dozen empty, let them ne continually washed and kept under, so that upon an emergency they are always ready: and if you want fresh saw dust in the bins, observe it is all *well dried* by a fire before you put it there. When you have done brewing, the tubs and pails should be turned up, leaving some *water* on their bottoms, which will keep them tight all the summer, and prevent their falling to pieces.

In having the care of the cheese for the parlour, let a broad hanging shelf be hung either in the *wine or strong beer cellar* for them, (the former would be more preferable,) and suffer no one to meddle with them ; and never let it, or the wine, spring-water, beer, or bread, be brought into the parlour above *one minute before they are wanted.* If you keep the cream cheese, put them between two dishes, and turn them every morning ; and *for all other cheese, have a rack or two made for them* in your cellar, for it will be a means of improving them daily. A large space should be left for the Cheshire cheeses ; and *nothing more improves th* than putting three or four on each *pipe of wine, and brushing and turning them every day.* Cheese of an inferior quality will become *rich, fine and mellow* by this method, and letting them be turned alternately.

P. S. As Capillaire is fine in ſpring water or milk, during the hot months, you have here a receipt to make it, with that of *Orgeat, Lemonade, Milk Punch,* and *Mead.* And if your family are in the habit of drinking *Punch,* never uſe any water unleſs it has *boiled*; let the ſugar, water and fruit be well mixed, before you put in the *ſpirits*; and to a large bowl, you may add *a good gill of old ſtrong beer,* for this mellows it *prodigiouſly,* and takes the heat off the ſpirits; and if you rub well all over each lump of ſugar you intend to uſe, upon the lemon and orange, it will give the punch a *fine rich flavour*; and then put a thin slice of lemon and orange peal into the bowl.

THE

COMPLETE FAMILY-BREWER:

OR THE

BEST METHOD

OF

BREWING OR MAKING ANY QUANTITY

OF GOOD

STRONG ALE & SMALL-BEER,

In the greatest Perfection,

FOR THE

USE OF PRIVATE FAMILIES,

FROM A PECK TO A HUNDRED QUARTERS OF MALT.

TOGETHER WITH

DIRECTIONS FOR CHOOSING GOOD MALT, HOPS, WATER, BREWING-VESSELS. CLEANING and SWEETENING FOUL CASKS, BREWING-VESSELS, &c.—TO MAKE NEW MALT LIQUOR DRINK STALE; WITH DIRECTIONS FOR BOTTLING.—AND THE MOST PROPER TIME FOR BREWING, &c. &c.

BY THOMAS THREALE, BREWER.

TO WHICH IS ADDED,

AN APPENDIX,

CONTAINING THE ART OF BREWING PORTER, AND MAKING BRITISH WINES.

LONDON:

PRINTED FOR M. JONES, No. 1, PATERNOSTER-ROW,

BY J. H. HART, 23, Warwick-Square.

1802.

PREFACE.

IT is hoped the following calculation will be thought a sufficient apology for publishing this Small Pamphlet:

The strong beer (or porter) costs, if bought at the public-houses in London, at least fourpence-halfpenny per pot, or quart, which is eighteen-pence per gallon; — the ale that is sold by the publicans of London, and the country in general, is upon an average eight pence per quart; — and the small beer, which is small indeed, three half-pence per quart, or sixpence per gallon. — London porter, in the country, is sold from 6*d.* to 8*d.* per quart.

A 2 The

The following statement will shew how much a family may save in one year by brewing their own beer:

One bushel of malt and one peck of hops will make six gallons of strong-beer, or ale, and twelve gallons of small beer:

	l.	*s.*	*d.*
Six gallons of strong beer, at 1*s.* 6*d.* per gallon	0	9	0
Twelve gallons of small beer, at 6*d.* per gallon	0	6	0
	0	15	0

On the contrary,

One bushel of malt	0	7	6
One pound of hops	0	1	6
	0	9	0

Which makes a saving of six shillings out of fifteen for your trouble of brewing, &c. A very valuable consideration to some families in these times, when all the necessary articles of life are sold at such an extravagant price; besides the advantage of knowing that what you drink is really

really good and nourishing, which is more than can in general be said of the liquor that is purchased ready brewed to your hands.

I have not added the coals, as the sale of the grain, yest, &c. will fully pay for them. The malt and hops I have set down at a full price, and few people use more than three quarters of a pound of hops, and some only half a pound; and, besides that, small beer is generally retailed out at twopence per quart.

As to the treacle-beer, I shall say very little; but let it speak for itself: I shall only observe this, that it is preferable to that sold at the chandler-shops in London; and I am persuaded they would have more custom if they were to sell it instead of the rot-gut stuff imposed on them by their brewers, under the name of small beer; and with this advantage, too, that they make it themselves for half the price.

THE COMPLETE FAMILY-BREWER.

THIS Little Pamphlet being intended principally for the use of private Families, it will be necessary to begin with Directions.

How to choose Good Malt.

Malt is chosen by its sweet smell, mellow taste, full flower, round body, and thin skin. There are two sorts in general used, — the pale and the brown. — The former is most used in gentlemen's houses and private families; the latter, in public brew-houses, as it seems to go farther, and makes the liquor high coloured. Others, again, mix one-third brown with two-thirds pale;

but this depends upon the liking of the drinkers. The sweetest malt is that which is dried with coak or cinders.

In grinding it, see that the mill be clean from dust, cobwebs, &c. and set so as to crush every grain, without grinding it to powder; for, you had better have some small grains slip through untouched than have the whole ground too small, which will cause it to cake together, so as you cannot get the goodness out of it.

Of Hops.

Hops are chosen by their bright green colour, sweet smell, and clamminess when rubbed between the hands.

Of Water for Brewing

Water out of rivers or rivulets is the best, except polluted by the melting of snow or land water, from clay or ploughed lands. Snow-water will take nearly one-fifth part more of malt to make the beer good. If you have no river-water, a pond that has a bottom not very muddy, and is fed by a spring, will do; for, the sun will soften and rarify it. Very hard water, drawn from a deep well into a wide cistern or reservoir, and exposed to the air or sun, in two or three days has been brewed with success, by the addition of malt. Rain-water comes next to river for brewing.—In short, all water that will raise a lather with soap is good for brewing.

Of

Of the Brewing-Vessels.

To a copper that holds thirty-six gallons, the mash-tun ought to be at least big enough to contain six bushels of malt and the copper of liquor, and room for mashing or stirring it: the under back, coolers, and working-tuns, may be rather fitted for the conveniency of the room than to a particular size; for, if one vessel be not sufficient to hold your liquor, you may take a second.

Of cleaning and sweetening Casks and Brewing-Vessels.

If a cask, after the beer is drunk out, be well stopped to keep out the air, and the lees remaining in it till you want to use it again, you will need only to scald it well, and take care of the hoops before you fill it; but, if air gets into a foul empty cask, it will contract an ill scent in spite of scalding. A handful of bruised pepper boiled in the water you scald with, will take out a little musty smell; but the surest way is to take out the head of the cask, and let the cooper shave and burn it a little, and then scald it for use; if you cannot conveniently have a cooper to the cask, get some stone-lime, and put about three pounds into a barrel, (and proportionably to smaller or larger vessels,) and put to it about six gallons of cold water, and bung it up and shake it about for some time, and afterwards scald it well; or, for want of lime, take a linen rag, and dip it in melted brimstone,

brimstone, fastening one end to the bung, then light the other, and let it hang on the cask. You must give it a little air, or else it will not burn; but keep in as much of the sulphur as you can. Scald it afterwards, and you will find no ill smell.

If you have new casks, before you fill them, dig places in the earth, and lay them half their depth, with their bung-holes downwards, for a week; and, after scalding them, you may venture to fill them.

Another way to proceed is, if your brewing-vessels are affected with any ill smell, to take unslacked lime and water, and with an old broom scrub the vessel whilst the water is hissing with the lime; afterwards, take all this lime and water away, put fresh water in the vessel, throw some bay or common salt into each, and let it stand a day or two; and, when you come to brew, scald your vessels, throw into them a little malt-dust or bran, and this will not only finish their sweetening, but stop them from leaking.

But, since there is so much trouble in getting vessels sweet after they have been neglected, you ought to make all thorough clean after brewing; and once a month you should fill your vessels with fair water, and let it off again in two or three days.

Of Mashing or taking your Liquor.

Suppose you take six bushels of malt, and two pounds of hops, and would make of it one barrel of strong and two barrels of small beer.

Heat

Heat your first copper of liquor for mashing, and strew over it a double handful of bran or malt, by which you will see when it begins to boil; for, it will break and curl, and then it is fit to be let off into the mash-tun, where it must remain till the steam is quite spent, and you can see your face in it, before you put in your malt: and then you begin to mash, stirring it all the while you are putting in the malt; but keep out about half a bushel dry, which you are to strew over the rest, when you have done stirring it, which will be as soon as you have well mixed it with the liquor, and prevented it from clodding.

After the dry malt is laid on, cover your mash-tun with the sacks or cloths, to prevent losing any spirit of the malt, and let it so remain for two hours. Meanwhile, have another copper of liquor hot; and, at two hours end, begin to let off your first wort into the under back; receive a pailful of the first running, and throw it again upon the malt. You will find that the malt has sucked up half of the first copper of liquor; and, therefore, to make up your quantity of wort for your strong beer, you must gradually dip out of the second copper, and strew bowl after bowl over the malt, giving it time to soak through, and keeping it running by an easy stream, till you perceive you have about forty gallons; which, in boiling and working, will be reduced to thirty-six.

If you throw into the under back (while you are letting off) about half a pound of hops, it will preserve it from foxing, or growing sour or ropy.

Your first wort being all run off, you must soften the tap of the mash-tun, and take a copper of of hot liquor for your second mashing, stirring up the malt as you did at first; and then cover it close for two hours more. Mean-while you fil lyour copper with the first wort, and boil it with the remainder of the two pounds of hops, for an hour and a half, and then lade it off into the coolers.

Contrive to receive the hops into a sieve, basket, or thin woolen bag that is sweet and clean; then immediately fill your copper with cold liquor: renew your fire under it; then begin to let off your second wort, and throw a handful of hops into the under back, for the same reason as before; you will want to lade a few bowls full of liquor over the malt to make up the copper full of second wort; and. when you have enough, fasten the tap and mash a third time after the same manner; and cover it close for another two hours: and then charge your copper with the second wort, boiling it for an hour with the same hops.

By this time you may shift your first wort out of the coolers into a working tun, to make room for the second wort to come into the coolers; and then your copper being empty, you may heat as much liquor as will serve you to lade over the malt, or, by this time, rather grains, to make up your third and last copper of wort, which must be boiled with the same hops over again; and then your coolers are discharged of your second wort, to make room for the third; and may be put together before you set them working.

If you would extract almost all the goodness of the malt in the first wort, by way of making

October

October beer, you must begin to let off soon after you have mashed, (by a small stream,) and throw it upon the malt again, pail after pail, for an hour, stirring it frequently in the mean time; and then let it all run off by a very small stream. But, when you have your quantity of strong beer, you must proceed in your second mashing, as before.

During the time of shifting your liquors out of the copper, it is of consequence to take care to preserve it from receiving damage by burning. You should always contrive to have the fire low; or else to damp it at the time of emptying, and be very expeditious to put in fresh liquor.

Of Working the Liquor.

In this, regard must be had to the water.— Liquor naturally grows warm with working; therefore, in mild weather, it should be cold before it be set on, but a little warm in cold weather. The manner of doing it is, to put some good sweet yest into a hand-bowl or piggin, with a little warm wort: then put the hand-bowl to swim upon the wort in the working-tun; and, in a little time, it will work out, and leisurely mix with the wort. And, when you find the yest has gotten hold of the wort, you must look after it frequently; and, if you perceive it begin to heat and ferment too fast, lade some of it out into another tub; and, when grown cold, it may be put back again: or, if you reserve some of the raw wort, you may check it leisurely

surely by stirring it with a hand-bowl. The cooler you work your liquor, the better; provided it does but work well.

If you happen to check it too much, you may forward its working, by filling a gallon stone bottle with boiling water, corking it close, and putting the bottle into the working-tun. An ounce or two of powdered ginger will have the same effect.

There is a variety of methods in managing liquors while they are working. In the north, they beat the yest of strong beer and ale once in two or three hours, for two or three days together.

This they reckon makes the drink more heady, but withal hardens it so as to be drinkable in two or three days; the last day of beating it in, (stirring the yest and beer together,) the yest, as it rises, will thicken; and then they take off part of the yest, and beat in the rest; which they repeat as often as it rises thick; and, when it has done working, they tun it up, so as it may just work out of the barrel.

Others, again, do not beat it in at all, but let their strong drink work about two days, or till they see the ferment is over; and then they take off the top yest; and, either by a tap near the bottom let it off fine, or else lade it out gently to leave the sediment and yest at the bottom. This way is proper for liquor that is to be drunk soon; but, if it be to keep, it will want the sediment to feed upon, and may probably grow stale, unless you make artificial lees. This you make of a quart of brandy, and as much flour

flour of wheat or beans as will make it into dough; put them in lumps into the bung-hole as soon as it has done working. Or else, take a pound of the powder of oister-shells, or of fat chalk, and mix it with a pound of treacle or honey, and put it in soon after it has done working.

It would add to the goodness, as well as fining, of your malt liquor, if you took two quarts of wheat or beans, and made them very dry and crisp in an oven, or before the fire, and boiled them in your first copper of wort. They would strain off with your hops, and might be put with them into the second copper.

Of the fining of Malt Liquors.

It is most desirable to have beer fine of itself, which it seldom fails to do in due time, if rightly brewed and worked; but, as disappointments some times happen, it will be necessary to know what to do in such cases.

Ivory-shavings boiled in your wort, or harts-horn-shavings put into your cask just before you bung it down, will do much towards fining and keeping your liquor from growing stale.

Isinglass is the most common thing made use of in fining all sorts of liquors; they first beat it well with a hammer or mallet, and lay it in a pail; and then draw off about two gallons of the liquor to be fined upon it, and let it soak two or three days; and, when it is soft enough to mix with the liquor, they take a whisk, and stir it about till it is all of a ferment, and white froth; and they fre-quently

quently add the whites and shells of about a dozen eggs, which they beat in with it, and put all together into the cask; then, with a clean mop-stick or some such thing, stir the whole together; and then lay a cloth or piece of paper over the bung-hole till the ferment is over, and then bung it up close; in a few days it will fall fine.

But, if you want to fine only a small quantity, take half an ounce of unslacked lime, and put it into a pint of water; stir it well together, and let it stand for two or three hours, or till the lime settle to the bottom; then pour the water off clear, and throw away the sediment; afterwards, take half an ounce of isinglass cut small, and boil it in the lime-water till it dissolves; then let it cool, and pour it into the vessel, &c.

Of recovering and preserving Malt Liquors.

Stormy weather, but especially thunder, will greatly affect your beer, and often ferments it, though brewed six months before. In such weather, you should examine your cellar, and draw your vent-pegs; and, where you perceive it upon the fret, draw out the bung, and let it remain some days till you are sure it is quiet. It is a fault to be too hasty in bunging up the liquor; it had better be a week too long out, than stopped an hour too soon. Were it not for preserving the colour of the liquor, some cherry brandy thrown into the bung-hole would stop it from fretting.

If

If your strong beer grows flat, you may quicken it by drawing off one gallon out of every ten, and boil it with as many pounds of honey as you boil gallons; and, when it is cold, put it to the rest, and stop it close.

A spoonful of the juice of the herb horehound, strained into a pitcher of stale beer, and covered close for two hours, will make it drink like new.

Or, if you would bottle beer that is stale and flat, you should contrive to do it when you have liquor working in your tun; and leave room in every bottle to hold the quantity of a coffee-cup, and fill them up with new drink out of the tun; then cork them, and in three days it will be very brisk, and drink pleasant; but you must not propose to keep it long; for, it will burst the bottles.

Of the Season for Brewing.

The season for brewing keeping-beer, is certainly best before Christmas; for, then your malt is in perfection, not having time to contract either a musty smell, dust, or weasels, (an insect that eats out the heart of the malt,) and the waters are then seldom mixed with snow; and then four pounds of hops will go as far as five in the spring of the year: for, you must increase in the quantity of hops as you draw towards summer. But, in short, choose moderate weather as much as you can for brewing; and, if you have a kindly cellar besides to keep your liquor in, that will not be much affected by extremity of heat or cold, you may reasonably expect great satisfaction in your brewery.

Avoid, as much as possible, brewing in hot weather; but, if you are necessitated to brew, make no more than for present drinking; for, it will not keep.

To make Alderberry Beer, or Ebulum.

Take a hogshead of the first and strong wort, and boil in the same one bushel of picked alderberries, full ripe: — strain off; and, when cold, work the liquor in the hogshead, and not in an open tun or tub; and, after it has lain in the cask about a year, bottle it, and it will be a most rich drink, which they call *ebulum*; and has often been preferred to port-wine, for its pleasant taste and healthful quality.*

N. B. — There is no occasion for the use of sugar in this operation; because the wort has strength and sweetness enough in itself to answer that end; but there should be an infusion of hops added to the liquor, by way of preservation and relish.

Some likewise hang a small bag of bruised spices in the vessel. — You may make a white ebulum with pale malt and white alderberries.

---

* It is well known, that a great quantity of this *beer* is sold annually in London for *port-wine*. — EDITOR.

To

To make improved, and excellent wholesome Purl.

Take Roman wormwood, two dozen; gentian-root, six pounds; calamas aromaticas, (or the sweet flag-root,) two pounds; a pound or two of galiengale-root; horse-radish, one bunch; orange-peel dried, and juniper-berries, each two pounds; seeds or kernals of Seville oranges, cleaned and dried, two pounds.

These being cut and bruised, put them into a clean but, and start your mild brown or pale beer upon them, so as to fill up the vessel, about the beginning of November, and let it stand till the next season; and make it thus annually.

To brew Strong Beer.

To a barrel of beer, take two bushels of wheat just cracked in the mill, and some of the flour sifted out of it. When your water is scalding-hot, put it into your mash-vat; there let it stand till you can see your face in it: — then put your wheat upon that, and do not stir it: — let it stand two hours and a half; then let it run into a tub that has two pounds of hops in it, and a handful of rosemary-flowers; and, when it has all run, put it into the copper, and boil it two hours: — then strain it off, setting it cooling very thin, and setting it working very cool: — Clear it very well before you set it working: — put a little yest to it; — when the yest begins to fall,

B 2 put

put it into your vessel, and put in a pint of whole wheat and six eggs; then stop it. — Let it stand a year, and then bottle it.

A good table-beer may be made by mashing again, after the preceding is drawn off; then let it stand two hours; and let that run, and mash again, and stir it as before. Be sure to cover your mash-vat well; mix the first and second running together.

To make China Ale.

To six gallons of ale, take a quarter of a pound or more of china-root, thin-sliced, and a quarter of a pound of coriander-seeds, bruised; hang these in a tiffany, or coarse linen bag, in the vessel, till it has done working; and let it stand fourteen days before you bottle; though the common sort, vended about town, is nothing more (at best) than ten-shilling beer, put up in small bottles, with a few spices, lemon-peel, and sugar.

To make Ale, or any other Liquor, that is too new or sweet, drink stale.

To do this to the advantage of health, put to every quart of ale, or other liquor, ten or twelve drops of the true spirits of salts, and let them be well mixed together; which they will soon do, by the subtle spirits penerating into all parts, and having their proper effect.

To

To recover sour Ale.

Scrape fine chalk, a pound, or more, as the quantity of liquor requires, put in a thin bag into the ale.

To recover Liquor that is turned bad.

If any liquor be pricked or fading, put to it a little syrup of clay, and let it ferment with a little barm, which will recover it: and, when it is well settled, bottle it up; put in a clove or two, with a lump of loaf sugar.

Directions for Bottling.

You must have firm corks boiled in wort, or grounds of beer: fill within an inch of the cork's reach, and beat it in with a mallet; then, with a small brass wire, bind the neck of the bottle; bring up the ends, and twist them over with a pair of pincers.

To make a Quarter of a Hogshead of Ale, and a Hogshead of Beer of coaked Malt.

Take five strike of malt, not ground too small; put in some boiling water, to cover the bottom of your mashing-vat, before you put in your malt: mash it with more boiling-water, putting in your malt at several times, that it may be sure to be all wet alike; cover it with a peck of wheat-bran; then let it stand thus mashed four hours; then draw off three gallons of wort, and pour it upon that you have mashed; so let it stand half an hour more, till it runs clear: then draw off all that will run, and make two quarts of it to begin to work up with the barm, which must be about a pint and a half; put in the two quarts of worts at three times to the barm: —you need not stir it till you begin to put in the boiled wort.

You will not have enough to fill your vessel at first: wherefore, you must pour on more boiling water, immediately after the other has done running, till you have enough to fill a quarter of a hogshead; and then pour on water for a hogshead of beer.

As soon as the ale-wort has run off, put a third part into the boiler: when it boils up, take off the scum, which you may put upon the grains for the small beer. When it is skimmed, put in a pound and a half of hops, having first sifted out the seeds. Then put in all the wort, and let it boil two hours and a half; afterwards strain it into two coolers, and let it stand to cool and settle; then put it to cool a little at a time to the barm and two quarts of wort, and beat it well together. Every time you put the wort in, be sure you keep the settling out.

Suppose you brew early on Thursday morning: you may turn it at nine or ten on Saturday morning.

Do not fill your vessel quite full, but keep about three gallons to put in when it has worked twenty-four twenty-four hours, which will make it work again.

As soon as it has done working, stop it up. Put the drink as cool as you can together; thus it will work well.

To make Treacle-Beer.

Boil two quarts of water, put into it one pound of treacle or molasses, stir them together till they are well mixed; then put six or eight quarts of cold water to it, and about a tea-cup full of yest or barm, put it up in a clean cask or stein, cover it over with a coarse cloth two or three times double, and it will be fit to drink in two or three days.

The second and third time of making, the bottom of the first beer will do instead of yest.

If you make a large quantity, or intend it for keeping, you must put in a handful of hops, and another of malt, for it to feed on; and, when done working, stop it up close.

The above is the best and cheapest way of making treacle-beer; though some people add raisins, bran, wormwood, spices, such fruit, &c. as are in season, but that is just as you fancy.

Indeed, many pleasant, cheap, and wholesome, drinks, may be made from fruits, &c. if they are bruised and boiled in water, before the treacle is added.

APPENDIX.

By way of an Appendix, I have added some some few particulars respecting the Art of Porter-Brewing, as it is practised in London; and to withdraw the mystic veil, for the benefit of society at large, and more particularly the lower classes: to point out how the artizan, the mechanic, the tradesman, and the cottager, may supply themselves and families with a beverage (retaining all the good qualities of porter and excluding all its noxious ones) infinitely more nutritive, and much cheaper.

The author has, also, added in this Appendix the *Art of making British Wines*, for the use of those families who may wish to manufacture their own wines as well as beer and ale. If this plan were practised in families, the author is certain they would find a great saving at the year's end; besides the benefit of having their wine good, and made to their own palate.

Receipt

Receipt for Porter-brewing.

WITH THE AVERAGE-PRICES OF THE DIFFERENT ARTICLES.

	l.	s.	d.
1 quarter of malt	3	0	0
8 pounds of hops	0	12	0
9 pounds of treacle	0	1	6
8 pounds of liquorice-root	0	5	6
8 pounds of essentia bina , ...	0	5	0
8 pounds of colour	0	5	0
Half an ounce of capsicum	0	0	3
2 ounces of Spanish liquorice	0	0	2
A quarter of an ounce of Creolus Indian Berry	0	0	2
2 Drachms of Salt of Tartar	0	0	1
¼ of an ounce of powdered alum and copperas, half and half, mixed . . .	0	0	1
3 ounces of ginger	0	0	3
4 ounces of slacked lime	0	0	1
1 ounce of linseed	0	0	0½
2 Drachms of cinnamon	0	0	1½
	4	10	3

The above ingredients will produce five barrels of good porter; which, if bought in London at the public-houses, will cost 13*l.* 10*s.* A saving of 8*l.* 19*s.* 9*d.* for your trouble of brewing, is an object of some consideration.

It is necessary that some of the above ingredients should be here explained.

1st.

1st. Essentia bina is eight pounds of moist sugar boiled in an iron vessel to a thick syrup, quite black and very bitter.

2nd. Colour, composed of eight pounds of moist sugar, boiled till it is between bitter and sweet, and which gives porter a fine mellow colour.

When you make the essentia and colour, the sugar is to be boiled sufficiently to make it liquid to pour off into your liquor. Add to it a little clean water, or lime-water, to bring it to a proper temper, and prevent it turning into a hard, dry, burnt, substance; which will be the case if suffered to stand until cold, as no water must be put to it before it is burnt enough.

After you have prepared these ingredients, put them to your first wort, and boil them together. Sugar, variously prepared, gives to porter strength, spirit, and body.

Linseed, ginger, cinnamon, lime-water, &c. are added at pleasure; being merely optional, and used solely to give flavour to the beer.

Heading, or *froth*, which landlords are so anxious to raise to please their customers, is a mixture (half and half) of alum and copperas ground into powder.

For the benefit of lodgers, and those who have not convenience or means of brewing-utensils, the following receipt is added for brewing one peck of malt:

Receipt.

	£.	s.	d.
1 peck of malt	0	1	10½
A quarter of a pound of liquorice-root,	0	0	2½

A

	l.	s.	d.
A quarter of a pound of Spanish liquorice	0	0	1
A quarter of a pound of essentia . .	0	0	3
A quarter of a pound of colour . . .	0	0	2½
Half a pound of treacle	0	0	1½
A quarter of a pound of hops	0	0	4½
Capsicum and ginger	0	0	6½
	0	3	8

Substitutes for Brewing-Vessels.

The kettle you use in washing, (which all persons must have,) that holds about two gallons and a half, will serve very well for a copper; a pail, (by boring a hole in the bottom of it,) for a mash-tub; and a washing-tub, an excellent vessel for the liquor to work in.

	l.	s.	d.
The above receipt will produce six gallons of good beer; which, if bought at the *Jolly Brewer*, or any other public house is	0	9	0
Brewed at Home	0	3	8
Leaving a clear Sum of . . . . for your trouble.	0	5	4

Who would not brew his own beer? —

The beer will be drinkable in six days, and be perfectly wholesome. — Reader, thou shouldst always remember Poor Richard's saying,

"Money saved is money got."*

* See Jones's Edition of Dr. Franklin's Works. — If thou hast never read this great philosopher's works, I will beg leave to recommend to thee to peruse them without farther delay.

RECEIPTS

OF

HOME-MADE

BRITISH WINES.

To make Raisin-Wine.

Take two hundred weight of raisins, stalks and all, and put them into a large hogshead; fill it with water: — let them steep a fortnight, stirring them every day. Then pour off all the liquor and press the raisins. Put both liquors together in a nice clean vessel that will just hold it; for, it must be full. Let it stand till it has done hissing, or making the least noise; then stop it close and let it stand six months. Peg it; and, if you find it quite clear, rack it off in another vessel; stop it close, and let it stand three months longer: then bottle it; and, when you use it, rack it off into a decanter.

To make Elder-Wine.

Pick the elder-berries when full ripe, put them into a stone jar, and set them in the oven, or a kettle

kettle of boiling water, till the jar is hot through; then take them out, and strain them through a coarse cloth, (wringing the berries,) and put the juice into a clean kettle. To every quart of juice put a pound of fine Lisbon sugar; let it boil, and skim it well. When it is clear and fine, pour it into a jar; when cold, cover it close, and keep it till you make raisin-wine; then, when you turn your wine, to every gallon of wine put half a pint of the elder-syrup.

To make Orange-Wine.

Take twelve pounds of the best powder-sugar, with the whites of eight or ten eggs well beaten, into six gallons of spring-water, and boil it three quarters of an hour. When cold, put into it six spoonfuls of yest, and the juice of twelve lemons, which being pared must stand with two pounds of white sugar in a tankard, and in the morning skim off the top, and then put it into the water; then add the juice and rinds of fifty oranges, but not the white parts of the rinds; and so let it work all together two days and two nights: then add two quarts of Rhenish or white wine, and put it into your vessel.

To make Orange-Wine with Raisins.

Take thirty pounds of new Malaga raisins picked clean, chop them small; take twenty large Seville oranges, ten of them you must pare as thin as for preserving; boil about eight gallons of soft

soft water till a third be consumed; let it cool a little: then put about five gallons of it hot upon your raisins and orange-peel, stir it well together; cover it up; and, when it is cold, let it stand five days, stirring it once or twice a day: then pass it through a hair-sieve, and with a spoon press it as dry as you can; put it in a runlet fit for it, and put to it the rind of the other ten oranges, cut as thin as the first; then make a syrup of the juice of twenty oranges with a pound of white sugar. It must be made the day before you turn it up: stir it well together, and stop it close. Let it stand two months to clear; then bottle it up. It will keep three years, and is better for keeping.

To make Elder-Flower Wine, very like Frontiniac.

Take six gallons of spring-water, twelve pounds of white sugar, six pounds of raisins of the sun chopped; boil these together one hour; then take the flowers of elder, when they are falling, and rub them off to the quantity of half a peck. When the liquor is cold, put them in; the next day, put in the juice of three lemons, and four spoonsful of good ale-yest. Let it stand covered up two days: then strain it off, and put it in a vessel fit for it. To every gallon of wine put a quart of Rhenish; and put your bung lightly on a fortnight; then stop it down close. Let it stand six months; and, if you find it is fine, bottle it off.

To

To make Gooseberry-Wine.

Gather your gooseberries in dry weather, when they are half ripe, pick them, and bruise a peck in a tub with a wooden mallet: then take a horse-hair cloth, and press them as much as possible, without breaking the seeds. When you have pressed out all the juice, to every gallon of gooseberries put three pounds of fine dry powder-sugar; stir it all together till the sugar is dissolved; then put it in a vessel or cask, which must be quite full. If ten or twelve gallons, let it stand a fortnight; if a twenty-gallon cask, five weeks. Set it in a cool place, then draw it off from the lees: clear the vessel of the lees, and pour in the clear liquor again. If it be a ten-gallon cask, let it stand three months; if a twenty-gallon, four months: then bottle it off.

To make Currant-Wine.

Gather your currants on a fine dry day, when the fruit is full ripe; strip them, put them into a large pan, and bruise them with a wooden pestle. Let them stand in a pan or tub twenty-four hours to ferment: then rub it through a hair-sieve, and do not let your hand touch the liquor. To every gallon of this liquor, put two pounds and a half of white sugar; stir it well together, and put it into your vessel. To every six gallons, put in a quart of brandy, and let it stand six weeks. If it is fine, bottle it; if it is not, draw it off as clear

as

as you can, into another vessel or large bottles; and, in a fortnight, bottle it in small bottles.

To make Cherry-Wine.

Pull your cherries when full ripe off the stalks, and press them through a hair-sieve. To every gallon of liquor put two pounds of lump-sugar beat fine; stir it together, and put it into a vessel; it must be full. When it has done working and making any noise, stop it close for three months, and bottle it off.

To make Birch-Wine.

The season for procuring the liquor from the birch-trees is in the beginning of March, while the sap is rising, and before the leaves shoot out; for, when the sap is come forward, and the leaves appear, the juice, by being long digested in the bark, grows thick and coloured, which before was thin and clear.

The method of procuring the juice is, by boring holes in the body of the tree, and putting in fossets, which are commonly made of the branches of elder, the pith being taken out. You may, without hurting the tree, if large, tap it in several places, four or five at a time; and, by that means, save from a good many trees several gallons every day; if you have not enough in one day, the bottles in which it drops must be corked close, and rosined or waxed: however, make use of it as soon as you can.

Take

Take the sap and boil it as long as any scum rises, skimming it all the time. To every gallon of liquor put four pounds of good sugar, and the thin peel of a lemon; boil it afterwards half an hour, skimming it very well: pour it into a clean tub; and, when it is almost cold, set it to work with yest spread upon a toast: let it stand five or six days, stirring it often. Then take such a cask as will hold the liquor; fire a large match dipped in brimstone, and throw it into the cask; stop it close till the match is extinguished. Turn your wine; lay your bung on light, till you find it has done working. Stop it close, and keep it three months; then bottle it off.

To make Quince-Wine.

Gather the quinces when dry and full ripe; take twenty large quinces, wipe them clean with a coarse cloth, and grate them with a large grater or rasp as near the core as you can, but none of the core. Boil a gallon of spring-water; throw in your quinces; let it boil softly about a quarter of an hour; then strain them well into an earthen pan on two pounds of double-refined sugar. Pare the peel of two large lemons, throw in and squeeze the juice through a sieve; stir it about till it is very cool; then toast a little bit of bread very thin and brown; rub a little yest on it; let it stand close covered twenty-four hours: then take out the toast and lemon, put it up in a keg, keep it three months, and then bottle it. If you make a twenty-gallon cask, let it stand six months

C before

before you bottle it; when you strain your quinces, you are to wring them hard in a coarse cloth.

To make Cowslip or Clary-Wine.

Take six gallons of water, twelve pounds of sugar, the juice of six lemons, and the whites of four eggs beat very well; put all together in a kettle; let it boil half an hour, and skim it very well. Take a peck of cowslips; if dry ones, half a peck; put them into a tub, with the thin peeling of six lemons; then pour on the boiling liquor, and stir them about; when almost cold, put in a thin toast baked dry and rubbed with yest. Let it stand two or three days to work. If you put in before you tun it six ounces of syrup of citron or lemons, with a quart of Rhenish wine, it will be a great improvement. The third day strain it off, and squeeze the cowslips through a coarse cloth; then strain it through a flannel bag, and turn it up. Lay the bung loose for two or three days to see if it works; and, if it does not, bung it down tight. Let it stand three months, then bottle it.

To make Turnip-Wine.

Take a great many turnips; pare, slice, and put them in a cider-press, and press out all the juice very well. To every gallon of juice have three pounds of lump-sugar. Have a vessel ready just big enough to hold the juice: put your sugar into a vessel; and also to every gallon of juice,

juice, half a pint of brandy. Pour in the juice, and lay something over the bung for a week, to see if it works: if it does, you must not bung it down till it has done working; then stop it close for three months, and draw it off in another vessel. When it is fine, bottle it off.

To make Raspberry-Wine.

Take some fine raspberries; bruise them with the back of a spoon; then strain them through a flannel bag into a stone jar. To each quart of juice put a pound of double-refined sugar: stir it well together, and cover it close. Let it stand three days, then pour it off clear. To a quart of juice put two quarts of white wine; bottle it off. It will be fit to drink in a week. — Brandy made thus is a very fine dram, and a much better way than steeping the raspberries.

THE END.

J. H. Hart, Printer, *Warwick-Square.*

Books printed for M. JONES, 1, *Paternoster-Row.*

CRITICAL INQUIRY into the MORAL WRITINGS of DR. JOHNSON: to which is added HUMOROUS DIALOGUES, between *Johnson* and *Boswell* in the SHADES.

"This is a well written and entertaining performance."—*Vide Monthly Review, May,* 1802.

"There is much good criticism upon Johnson's works in this "Inquiry. In the Humorous Dialogues, the manners of John-"son and Boswell are intimated with success."—*Antij. Rev. May,* 1802.

THE HERMIT OF THE ALPS, a moral tale, from the German, by J. Richardson, Esq. *Price* 1*s.*

LORD BACON'S ESSAYS, moral, political, and economical, with an elegant portrait. *Price* 6*s. boards.*

LORD BACON'S MISCELLANEOUS WTITINGS, philosophical, moral, &c. with an elegant representation of his monument at St. Alban's. *Price* 6*s.* 6*d. boards.*

LORD BACON'S WORKS, Vol. I. to IV. *Price* 1*l.* 4*s. boards.*

LOCKE'S THOUGHTS ON EDUCATION, 32*s*, divided under heads, *Price* 2*s.* 6*d. boards.*

LOCKE'S CONDUCT OF THE UNDERSTANDING, same size, being a companion to the above, *Price* 2*s. boards.*

DR. FRANKLIN'S WORKS, 2 vol. small 8vo. consisting of his life, written by himself; Essays, humorous, moral, &c. embellished with a fine portrait of the author. *Price* 8*s. boards.*

MASON'S SPIRITUAL TREASURY, new edition, in two large vol. 8vo. with elegant portraits of the Author and his Son, H. C. MASON, M. A. *Price* 16*s. boards.*

MASON'S BELIEVER'S POCKET-COMPANION, *Price* 1*s. boards.*

——— SCRIPTURAL PRAYERS, a new edition, with portrait of the author. *Price* 1*s. bound.*

——— CRUMBS FROM THE MASTER'S TABLE, *Price* 1*s. bound.*

——— HISTORY OF JESUS, for the Instruction of Children, *Price* 1*s.*

——— COMPANION TO THE SABBATH, 2 vol. 7*s.*

——— COMMUNICANT, *Price* 2*s.* 6*d.*

——— WORKS, publishing in Numbers, *Price* 1*s. each.*

CHRISTIAN REMEMBRANCER, a new edition, *Price* 3*s.* 6*d.*

THE ADVANTAGE AND DISADVANTAGE OF THE MARRIAGE STATE, *Price* 1*s,*

CAMBRAY ON CHARITY, *Price* 4*s.* 6*d.*

———'s PIOUS THOUGHTS, *Price* 1*s.*

——————— REFLECTIONS, *Price* 1*s,*

LADY PENNINGTON'S ADVICE to her DAUGHTERS, *Pr.* 2*s.* 6*d.*

THE FARMER'S BOY, a novel, by Miss Gunning, in 4 vol. *Price* 16*s. boards.*

LADY HUNTINGTON'S HYMNS, a new edition, with all the Supplements, and embellished with a portrait of her Ladyship, engraved by Hopwood, *fine,* 3*s.* 6*d. neatly bound.*

THE
Compleat *English* Brewer,
OR, THE
WHOLE ART and MYSTERY
OF
BREWING,
In all its various Branches,
CONTAINING

Plain and easy Directions for Brewing ALL Sorts of Malt Liquors in the *greatest* Perfection, from the smallest to the largest Quantities.

ALSO

Instructions for the Choice of Barley and Hops, and all other Ingredients and Utensils used in Brewing.

Together with the very best Methods of *Casking*, *Cellaring*, *Fining*, *Bottling*, *Curing* and *Recovering faulty or damaged Liquors*.

The whole made easy to every Capacity, and calculated not only for the use of PUBLICANS in general, but PRIVATE FAMILIES in particular.

By GEORGE WATKINS,
Who has practised Brewing in all its Branches, upwards of Thirty Years.

LONDON:
Printed for J. COOKE, at Shakespear's Head, in Pater-noster Row, MDCCLXVII.

PREFACE.

THE ſuperior excellence of malt-liquor above wine, in point of wholeſomeneſs, and the conſideration of its being a product of our own kingdom, are reaſons why every man who wiſhes well to his fellow-creatures and his country, ſhould promote, to the beſt of his power, the eſtimation and conſumption of it. The landed intereſt in this kingdom cannot but be affected very conſiderably by the quantity of malt-liquors for which there is a demand; and more now than at another time, becauſe the diſtillery is prevented from the free uſe of grain. Our hearty anceſtors knew no other wine, but that from corn or from the apple; and, if we

A 2 enquire

enquire into their conſtitutions, we ſhall find them, I am apt to believe, better than our own.

As evident as it is, that the general intereſt of our country is concerned in the queſtion, whether our tables ſhall be ſupplied from the grain our own fields produce, or the vineyards of ſtrangers, or our enemies; yet all the pleading in the world will be ineffectual, ſo long as wine is pleaſant, and beer leſs agreeable. Therefore he who would ſupercede, in ſome meaſure, the uſe of wine, by puting malt-liquor in its place, muſt truſt to a knowledge in the ſubject, not to arguments: the beſt of theſe will be received with a deaf ear; but the leaſt advance in the improvement of the rival liquor will be ſure to have its effect.

THAT our malt-liquors may be greatly improved is certain; for at preſent they are generally made either

either by ignorant or intereſted people. Thoſe who brew in the common way in the country, for their own families, make but a coarſe liquor; and as to the publick brewers, who regard the look and flavour of their drink, and nothing elſe, they put in ingredients which render it unwholeſome. The art of brewing is not known in families, and is not practiſed by brewers with that ſimplicity we could wiſh. It appeared, therefore, to the author of this little treatiſe, that it might be uſeful in many reſpects, to lay before the private family the beſt ſecrets which the brewers keep carefully to themſelves; and to lay down the certain principles of this eaſy operation, in a way that every body may underſtand them.

A good ſeaſon, good malt, good hops, and a proper kind of water, are the requiſites without which fine beer can never be made: but theſe are all in the perſons power

A 3 who

who brews ever ſo ſmall a quantity; and with theſe, and cleanlineſs, which is as neceſſary in the brew-houſe as in the dairy, there will be no fear but that the obſervance of the rules here laid down, will be re-warded with all the ſucceſs that can be deſired; and that every family may have, with little trouble, and at a ſlight expence, that barley-wine, as Cæſar calls it, in a degree of per-fection, that ſhall put the breweries of the wine-cooper out of counte-nance. Thoſe who ſet out amiſs, have nothing to conſider, but how to diſguiſe faults, or recover imperfec-tions; and the common books of brewery abound with receipts to this purpoſe. But it is always better to prevent evils than to cure them; and no drink of the malt kind, will ever be ſo good, as that which is made merely and only from that ingredient, with the hop and water.

UPON

Upon the whole, whoever will ſet about brewing, with the proportions of the ingredients we have directed, with a careful hand, clean utenſils, and proper veſſels, will be able, at leaſt, to equal the drink he meets with in the beſt houſes; probably to exceed it: and, if he will be very heedful of the management of the hop, to boil it little, but ſteep it well before-hand, he will find his drink ſecure in the great article of keeping. This management of the hop is one very great conſideration: and we ſhall cloſe this prefatory admonition, with one more invariable rule, which is, That whoever would have their ſtrong and ſmall beer both good, muſt brew them ſeparately, and not together.

THE

CONTENTS.

CHAP. XXIX.

CHAP. XXX.

CHAP. XXXI.

CHAP. XXXII.

CHAP. XXXIII.

CHAP. XXXIV.

CHAP. XXXV.

CHAP. XXXVI.

CHAP.

 CONTENTS.

CHAP.

CHAP. LIII.

THE

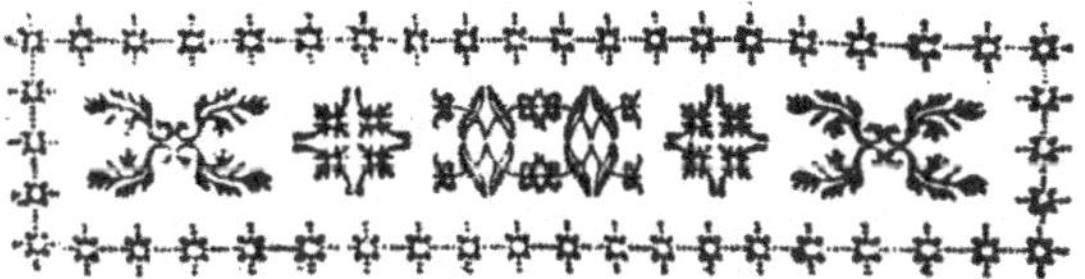

THE ART and MYSTERY OF BREWING.

INTRODUCTION.

THE making of good malt-liquor remains a ſecret in the hands of a few perſons; and, notwithſtanding the printing of many treatiſes, the public are yet wholly unacquainted with it. The Art of Brewing has hitherto ſeemed, like the Art of Gardening, a thing which many pretended to

B teach,

teach, but which none, except an accuſtomed hand, could practiſe with ſucceſs. Perhaps the myſtery in both caſes is on the eve of being brought to light. Certainly, I perſuade myſelf, that, by my own experience, and by carefully obſerving the practice of ſuch as brew well, I have informed myſelf of ſeveral leſſer articles, which never were yet publiſhed, but on which the ſucceſs of the work entirely depnds: and perhaps any one who will follow the ſame path, will do the public equal ſervice in the other article.

Upon the ſtrength of theſe obſervations, and the certainty of ſome practice, I hope to lay down, in a plainer manner than has hitherto been done, the general rules of brewing; and to direct even the leaſt parts of the operation in ſuch a way that all ſhall underſtand them: ſo that every one ſhall be able to brew good, wholeſome and pleaſant drink, and

and alſo to keep it in that order, without the addition of hurtful ingredients.

The old writers are all very deficient on this head; for the art in their time was not arrived at its perfection: and among the moderns few have written on it with clearneſs. There is a great deal of practical knowledge in the writings of ELLIS; but it is ſo mixed with idle opinions, that few of his readers can ſeparate what is worth their notice: Mr. COMBRUNE deſerves all the praiſe his patron has beſtowed on him; but he is philoſophical more than practical: And the improvements of the DUBLIN SOCIETY are excellent; but they relate only to a part of the buſineſs. Therefore, notwithſtanding all that has been done, a plain, compleat, and practical treatiſe is yet wanting: and this, ſupported by experience, is what we here propoſe to lay before the reader.

B 2 Of

Of the Ingredients in Brewing.

THE natural and proper ingredients in malt-liquors are only three, WATER, MALT, and HOPS. Every one thinks he underſtands theſe; and yet there are ſuch differences in every one of them, that, without a much more ſtrict attention than is uſually paid to them, good drink cannot be brewed, unleſs by chance: and this will not happen once in fifty trials.

CHAP. I.

Of Water.

WATER may be diſtinguiſhed into four kinds, SPRING, RIVER, RAIN, and POND; and what is the worſt in appearance often makes the beſt drink.

No water can be fouler than that of the THAMES, yet the clear-
eſt

eſt porter is brewed with it. Many have ſaid no other but Thames water would make this ſpecies of drink: but that is plainly an error; for even in London there are porter-brewers ſerved from the New River: however, none is better for it than that of the Thames: and in moſt caſes the very pureſt and fineſt water is, for brewing, the worſt of all.

Our forefathers brewed their ſtrong pale October with WELL WATER; but the expence in malt was very great, and the beer would have been wholeſomer and better if they had uſed river-water. The common foul water of large rivers, which differs little from that of ponds, would not have done; but the water of a clear rivulet beſt of all.

This may in ſome meaſure ſerve as a direction to the brewer in general terms; and he will find it true, that very ſoft water, ſuch as rain-water, and that of ponds, and very hard, ſuch as that of ſprings and wells, are proper in but a few caſes: and that for high-coloured drink, river-water is the beſt; and for the pale kinds, that of brooks or rivulets, with a ſwift current. He cannot always have this exact choice, but he muſt come as near it as he can..

CHAP. II.

Of the Differences of Malt.

ALL common malt is made of barley, and owes its difference to the manner of making and of drying. There are malts made of wheat, of oats, and even of beans; but we are here ſpeaking of the common kinds, which are all of barley. Theſe may be arranged under three heads; the BROWN, the PALE, and that middle kind which is called AMBER. The malt with which porter is brewed, is of the brown

brown kind; and is higher dried than any other. It is to be ſold at the ſame places with the reſt, under the name of porter-malt: and, what is very particular, it is made of an inferior kind of barley. The degree of fire with which it is dried gives that agreeable taſte and colour; and the art of the brewer, who thoroughly underſtands his buſineſs, makes that peculiar drink from it; not the water or any other ingredient. Great dealers have opportunities of great experience; and what they ſee wrong in one brewing, they can make right in another. This is the whole ſecret: what has been hitherto wanting, is the publiſhing the reſult of their experience.

The difference of the three malts is owing to the degree of fire, and the time allowed to dry them. The pale malt is dried very ſlow, and with a ſmall fire; the brown is done quick; and the amber is of a middle quality; dried with a moderate degree of time and heat. In general, the brown malts are to be brewed with the softest waters, because these best take out their strength and flavour: the pale malts should be brewed with spring-water, to preserve their fine colour; and the amber with a midling water, such as that of clear small rivers.

Which ever kind of malt be used, it may be judged by these methods as to its goodness. 1. By its lightness, which may be thus known. Take a little of it in the hand, carefully considering its weight in comparison of barley; for, when made as it should be, it is much lighter than the barley: and the lighter it is, provided it be sound, the better. 2. To judge of this more exactly, chuse out some fine sound and entire grains of the malt, and put them into a glass of pump-water. If the malt be good, they will swim on the surface. Barley sinks in in water; and if the malt be not well made, it will ſink in the like manner. This is a trial of the ſame nature with the firſt, but more accurate. 3. Chuſe a fine grain of the malt, and draw it hard over an oak board, croſs-wiſe of the grain: if it be good malt, there will be a white line upon the board like a mark of chalk.

The ſmell may after this be conſulted; for ſometimes malt, though well dried, has a ſcent from the fuel, or from foul water uſed in the ſteeping. It ſhould be perfectly free from this; and if ſweet, light, and anſwering to theſe ſeveral characters, we may be aſſured it is in perfection.

For the ſake of ſuch as are inclined to make their own malt, I ſhall here add the method of doing it, and the differences of the grain from which it is to be made.

B 5 CHAP.

CHAP. III.

Of chuſing proper Barley for making of Malt.

THE principal ingredient in brewing being the malt, and this being a preparation of barley, it is fit we begin with examining the nature of that grain; and the methods of bringing it into the ſtate of malt.

Gentlemen in the country, who are curious in their malt-liquor, may bring it to the higheſt poſſible perfection, by beginning in this manner at the very ſource, that is, with a right choice of the grain: and the knowledge of the rules by which this is to be choſen, will alſo be uſeful to thoſe who, not having theſe opportunities, buy their malt in the uſual way: ſince the ſame characters which diſtinguiſh the excellence of that made at home, will ſerve alſo as marks by which common

mon purchaſers may know the degree of goodneſs in what is ſold.

We have two or three kinds of barley raiſed in England; but the common long-eared ſort is the beſt and fitteſt for making malt. The greater is the perfection of the barley, the finer will be the malt. The fineſt and moſt perfect of this kind is ſuch as has grown upon a light rich loam, and has been raiſed from ſeed obtained by exchange from a diſtant farm, and different ſoil. The prime ſeed of ſuch a crop ſhould be ſelected for making of malt: it ſhould be freſh, heavy, large, and perfectly ſound, and ſuch as has ſuffered no accident from wet in the field, nor from dampneſs in the mow.

To the country-gentleman who manages ſome of his own land, there will be very little trouble, and no loſs, in thus chuſing the beſt of his produce for the ſupply of his cellar: and thoſe who make their own malt, and do not raiſe the grain themſelves, ſhould be careful to pick ſuch as is here directed in the market. If there ſhould be a trifle of difference in the price, it ſhould never be grudged, for it is nothing in compariſon of the advantage it will be to the liquors. We propoſe to give the beſt and moſt perfect method of brewing, and would not have our inſtructions fail for want of a little care in the firſt articles.

C H A P. IV.

Of making the Barley into Malt.

THE right kind of barley being choſen, no care can be too great in the making it into malt.

The firſt operation is the covering it with water, to ſoak it in the ciſtern; for this purpoſe the clear water of a running brook or ſmall river ſhould be choſen; or, if ſuch cannot be had,

had, pump-water muſt be taken; but then it muſt ſtand expoſed to the air four and twenty hours before it is uſed. If muddy river-water, or pond-water, be employed for ſteeping the barley, it gets a taint which it will never afterwards recover. The firſt impreſſion upon the grain is made by the water wherein it is ſteeped; and, if this be foul or ill-taſted, the ſame flavour will be communicated to the drink, whatever other care is uſed.

When the barley is thrown into the water, there ſhould be two hands-breadth of water above it, for leſs will not ſoak it properly. The generality of the corn will ſink; but, after a good ſtirring, there will ſome ſwim on the ſurface: theſe are bad grains. They ſhould be ſkimmed off: they will ſerve poultry or the hogs, but they will never make good malt.

In this water the barley is to lie about three days and nights. The difference

difference of the barley will make a difference of twelve hours or more in this matter; for the beſt ſoaks ſooneſt. But about what is here named as the general ſtandard: to know when it is ſoaked enough, take up one corn from the middle of the quantity, and hold it ſteadily between the fore-finger and thumb of the right-hand, by the two ends; preſs it gently, and the ſoftneſs will ſhew whether it is enough. If it continues firm upon preſſing, and the ſkin does not break, it muſt lie longer; if it cruſhes together, and feels mellow, and the ſkin cracks, it is enough. It muſt then be ſuffered to remain no longer in the water, for it would now begin to looſe part of its ſweetneſs.

The grain being ſoaked enough, the water is to be drawn leiſurely from it. After this it is to be put into a hutch, and lie together thirty two hours: after this it is to be turned thoroughly up once in ſix hours

hours on the floor: when it begins to ſpire, it muſt be turned every four hours with great care; and muſt be ſpread thin in a kind of beds on the floor, to prevent its ſpiring or ſhooting too faſt, but ſtill in ſuch thickneſſes in the beds as will preſerve moiſture enough to make it continue ſhooting in this gradual manner. When it is ſhot enough, it muſt be turned once in two hours; and the root will then ſoon wither. After this it muſt be laid thicker; and turned now and then. The care is, that the root does not grow any more; nor the ſpire ſhoot out at the oppoſite end: but then there is alſo danger of mouldineſs from this degree of damp without growth; and this is equally to be avoided; the frequent turning is the great article; and the workman muſt take care to keep a clean floor.

When the malt is made thus far without any accident, it is the common

mon practice to lay it on the kiln at once: but the true way is, to gather it all up in one heap, and then let it lie twelve hours. After this it is to be turned; and this is to be repeated every five hours, till it has been done four times. The malt will be then ready for the kiln; on which it will be dried in a few hours. As ſoon as it is dry, it muſt be removed from the kiln, and ſpread thin, that it may cool and harden at leiſure. This compleats the malt, and it is fit for uſe. There is no great difficulty in the making it; but thoſe who do not chuſe that trouble, will ſtill find the uſe of underſtanding how it is done; for upon the right management of theſe ſeveral articles depends the goodneſs of the malt that is offered to ſale; or upon the ill conduct of ſome of the articles its faults. If it has not been ſufficiently ſteeped in the firſt water, there will be a hardneſs in the whole grain; if bad water has

been

been uſed, it will have a muddy ſmell; if it has been ſuffered to ſhoot from the point oppoſite to the root, which is what the maltſters call acroſpiring, it will be poor, thin, light, and huſky: but if all the care here directed has been taken, it will be tender, ſweet, and mellow; and will have all the good characters we have given for the choice of malt.

The time of drying of malt varies according to the kind intended to be made, for the difference of colour depends on the drying quick or ſlow. For brown malt, four hours will be ſufficient, becauſe of the briſkneſs of the fire that is uſed. For amber malt, the fire being ſmaller, there will require about ſeven hours: and for the pale malt, the fire being very weak, the time will amount to twelve.

Thus, from the ſame parcel, either of theſe kinds may be made only by the different degree of fire.

CHAP.

CHAP. V.

Of the Hop.

THE next article is the choice of the hop; and in this there is as much care to be uſed as in either of the former. The ſoundneſs, the colour, and the ſcent, are to determine this choice principally: but I have found a great deal alſo to depend upon the internal condition.

He that would brew good drink, muſt look at no hops that have not the two great requiſites, of a good colour, and fine flavour; and, when theſe recommend them, he ſhould tear one or two open, and examine the ſeeds. The leafy part of the hop is only a kind of fine fragrant covering for theſe; and the ſeeds have alſo their value: theſe will be either perfect or imperfect, or even wholly wanting within, according to the time

time at which the hops were gathered; and according to the care uſed in drying them.

If the hop has been gathered too young, the ſeeds will be ſmall, ſhrivelled, and almoſt taſteleſs: if it has hung too long, or if it has been careleſsly cured, they will be fallen out.

When the hop has been gathered at a right degree of ripeneſs, and has been carefully dried, theſe ſeeds will be found under the ſcales in a conſiderable quantity, and they will be full, and well-taſted. This is a great article in the value of the hop, though it has been miſtaken by ſome writers; and in general is little regarded, except by the moſt judicious.

The newer the hop is, always the better it will prove; for the fineſt part of its flavour is loſt in ſome degree in keeping, though it be ever ſo carefully preſerved. Older hops may make beer that will keep very well;

well; but it will want the delicate flavour which the freſh ones give. The ſame fine flavour may be alſo loſt by over-boiling, though the hop has originally been ever ſo good. This will be ſhewn hereafter. Upon the whole, the hop ſhould be new, light, perfectly clean, free from any ill ſmell, and ſhould have its own fine fragrant flavour and agreeable bitter in perfection.

The difference in price between the beſt and the poorer kinds is not worthy to be conſidered, when we recollect the vaſt difference in the beer.

Having thus acquainted ourſelves with the nature and qualities of the ſeveral ingredients, we are to conſider the liquor that is propoſed to be made of them; and the methods by which, according to thoſe qualities, it may be obtained in the greateſt perfection.

CHAP.

CHAP. VI.

The Purpose of Brewing.

WHAT we propofe in brewing is, to obtain an infufion of the malted corn, impregnated with all its agreeable qualities; and not loaded with fuch parts of it as are unpleafant or unwholefome: to this we add flavour from the hop; and the fame ingredient gives it the quality of keeping.

What we expect and defire to obtain from the malt, is its agreeable balfamic quality; and from the hop its light bitternefs, and its delicate flauour. This was always the intent and purpofe of brewing; but it has in general been attempted in an irregular and injudicious manner. By long foaking in hot water, that is, by too long mafhing, we have been accuftomed to draw from the malt, befide its pure balfamic fpirit, its heavy

heavy earthy parts, which have overpowered the others; and, by boiling the hop a long time in the wort, we have been uſed to evaporate that fine part, on which its high flavour depends; preſerving only its heavy and diſagreeable bitter. Thus, inſtead of a mild, light, cordial, and balſamic liquor, ſuch as is propoſed to be made by brewing, we have had a heavy, heady, harſh, and auſtere drink, which has brought on thoſe very diſorders that the other would have cured.

Every art has its proper principles; and the better theſe are underſtood, the more ſucceſsfully the art itſelf will be practiſed. We hope to explain thoſe of brewing in a clear and plain, as well as certain manner; and, upon that regular knowledge of the ſubject, to direct the practice, in a manner that all may underſtand, and that will be certain to make the beſt, the pleaſanteſt, and

the

the wholesomest liquors of the several kinds and denominations.

CHAP. VII.

The Principles of Brewing.

WE are to obtain the finest and best qualities of the malt: now all the parts of plants give their fine qualities to water by a light infusion; and, if too much heat, or too much mashing them together be used, the coarser parts are also drawn out, and these drown the finer: the liquor is no longer of the same nature, taste, or flavour; and the very intent of what we are about is lost, by overstraining the means. There cannot be a plainer instance of this than we see every day in tea; we desire to make from this herb a pleasant, light, and cordial liquor; and for that purpose we pour hot water upon the leaves: this, after standing a very little time, produces what we we deſire; but if we boil the leaves in the water, or boil the liquor after we have made it by infuſion, either way we ſpoil it: in boiling the clear liquor, all the light and pleaſant part is loſt, and what remains is rough and nauſeous; and if we boil the tea itſelf in the water, we obtain a medicine not a pleaſant drink. If we only keep the leaves and the water too long together without boiling, and bruiſe and maſh them about, we obtain in the ſame manner a heavy, coarſe, and diſagreeable infuſion, that has nothing of the pleaſantneſs nor refreſhing quality of tea properly made.

Theſe are facts ſo plain that no one can conteſt them: they may be all applied in the ſame manner to an infuſion of malt for the making of beer; and that with greater force. Malt is a vegetable ſubſtance as well as tea; and it will part with its qualities to hot water as freely as tea; nay more freely, becauſe of the

preparation

preparation it has already undergone in making it into this form. It is therefore that boiling water is not required, nor is proper for it. In the ſame manner the hop is a vegetable ſubſtance, that will give its agreeable flavour, and fine bitter, readily to hot water, and needs not long boiling in it; nor indeed will bear it without damage. Some boiling it requires, becauſe the liquor into which it is put is not thin and pure as water, but is already impregnated with the malt: but, for the reaſons already given, the leſs boiling it has the better.

As the malt will readily give its virtues and beſt qualities to water, we ſhould no more let it ſtand too long in it; nor bruiſe and beat it about in it, than we ſhould tea: and as the leſs boiling the hop has, the better the drink will be, we ſhould uſe whatever methods will beſt anſwer the purpoſe of making it give its virtue by a little boiling.

C We

We know, if any plant, leaf, or flower, be firſt ſteeped or infuſed in the water, and then boiled, a few minutes boiling will extract its virtues as perfectly as an hour would have done if it had been at once put into the water, and made to boil: therefore we ſhould by all means ſoak or infuſe the hop ſome time in the wort before it is put with it into the copper.

Upon theſe plain principles, which are certain in themſelves, and which practice and experience confirm in this very article, it will be eaſy to make a great improvement in the article of brewing: for we ſee by them that the malt ſhould not be left a long time in the maſh-tub; but that the liquor on the contrary ſhould be drawn off after about three hours, when it has taken up all the fine qualities of the ingredient; and that we ſhould not beat it about in the maſh, becauſe that will make the liquor coarſe. In the ſame manner we we ſhould put the hops in a bag into the tub, which catches the liquor as it runs from the maſh-fat; and by this means they will be ſo well ſoaked, that a very little time will ſerve for boiling them in the copper.

Theſe two regulations will improve our brewing in general in a very great degree; and, inſtead of adding to the trouble or expence, will be a real ſaving of both.

Whatſoever can abate the time of boiling the wort, will be doubly uſeful in the brewings of private families; becauſe their coppers being ſmall, the effect of the boiling is much greater in the waſte of the liquor, and evaporation of its ſpirituous part. In large coppers the evaporation is much leſs in proportion in equal time, and therefore the beer ſuffers leſs than in the ſmall; and this is one great reaſon, though it be not regarded, why the brewers can brew better beer with the ſame quantity of malt, than other perſons can for themſelves. Another great reaſon of their advantage is, that they brew the ſeveral kinds ſeparate: and in this it will be well worth the while of private families to imitate them; for ſmall beer which is made of the laſt runnings after ſtrong, is never nearly equal to what is made but with a moderate quantity of the freſh ingredients alone.

CHAP. VIII.

The Utenſils for Brewing.

HAVING given this general idea of the nature of the ingredients, and the principles of making beer, it will be proper that we now conſider the veſſels and implements with which it is to be performed. Theſe make what is called the furniture of the brew-houſe; and, when they are underſtood in every part, the particular directions for

for brewing will be plain, and familiar to the reader.

The convenience of water is firſt to be conſidered: and as it will be proper, if poſſible, to have both kinds, there ſhould be conveniencies accordingly, a pump for ſpring water, and pipes for the river. We ſuppoſe the perſon ſituated where there are regular conveyances of water by common pipes, as the New River, Thames water, or the like, in London; otherwiſe there muſt be the expence of carriage of the river water: but in general the ſpring-water may be had upon the ſpot; and the nearer the well is to the brew-houſe the better.

A good leaden pump ſhould be placed in the brew-houſe; and there ſhould be a pipe to it, from the pipes of ſoft water, which ſhould run juſt by the copper at a ſmall height above it, and ſhould have a cock to open directly into the copper. This will ſave a vaſt deal of trouble; and thus,

C 3 as

as it will be eaſy to fill the copper with either kind alone, or with a mixture of both, there will be always the means of brewing any kind of malt at pleaſure; or indeed mixtures of any two may be thus managed as readily.

If the deſign be to brew high-dried malt, the river-water from the cock is to be let in alone; if pale malt is the kind to be uſed, the pump-water anſwers the purpoſe alone; or if amber malt, a mixture of the two. In the ſame manner any mixture at pleaſure of the pale and brown malts may be ſuited with a proper water, by mixtures of the pump and river-water: and this we ſhall aſſure the brewer, that although the cuſtom is to uſe one or other of theſe malts alone, the pleaſanteſt and beſt drinks of all are to be made by a mixture of the ſeveral kinds. Of this we ſhall ſpeak hereafter.

The

The copper muſt be proportioned in ſize to the quantity that will uſually be brewed; and it will be convenient to have it larger, rather than ſmaller, than the expected neceſſity. It ſhould be placed on an eminence, the floor being raiſed for that purpoſe where it ſtands. The beſt covering for the floor is that hard Dutch brick uſed for ovens; and there ſhould be a drain from one part, which opens into the common ſewer. By the means of this regulated height, all the following good purpoſes will be anſwered. The fire will burn briſker and better than if it lay lower; there will be no ſlop by waſte or ſpilling, becauſe the deſcent of the ground will carry all down immediately, and the drain will convey it away at once to the ſewer: then the brick-pavement will admit no wet to ſoak, ſo that all will be dry about the copper: finally, as the height favours a clear conveyance to the maſh-tubs

C 4 and

and coolers, there may be an arm carried from the copper to theſe, to let all the liquor out by a turn of a cock, and ſave the labour of ladling it, according to the old method. The copper muſt be ſo placed, that the ſmoak ſhall have an eaſy and free current up the chimney; and thus the brew-houſe will be always ſweet and dry, the whole buſineſs will be carried on with pleaſure, and the maſter may look in from time to time without diſguſt. This is a very eſſential conſideration; for, however diligent and intelligent ſervants are, there is no advantage like the eye of their maſter.

If the copper cannot be placed high enough for an arm to run to the maſh-tubs and coolers, there ſhould be a little braſs pump faſtened to the inſide of the copper, by which the water or wort can be pumped into the veſſels, through ſmall troughs; for this is not a tenth part of the trouble of the old way of ladling out; and

and it anſwers alſo better, becauſe of the greater regularity of the heat.

The maſh-tub ſhould be large. Suppoſe the copper to hold a hogſhead, the maſh-tub ſhould be big enough to maſh a quarter of malt with convenience. It ſhould be round, and not over deep; and over its bottom there ſhould be laid a falſe bottom, which may ſerve as a ſtrainer; when, by opening a caſk placed below it, the wort is drawn off into the receiver.

The receiver ſhould alſo be a round tub, ſhallower than the maſh-tub, and lined throughout bottom and ſides with thin milled lead. This is a vaſt advantage to the brewing, for the lead is eaſily kept perfectly clean, and is incapable of getting any bad ſcent or taſte, as will ſometimes happen to wood in ſpite of the beſt care. The cold nature of the lead ſerves alſo to cool the liquor the more quickly, which is a great article in this veſſel. The maſh-tub is to be placed ſo high as to leave room for this to move under it, becauſe that will give the convenience of letting out the wort from the maſh-tub into it, and of conveying it back again eaſily into the copper. The beſt method of doing this is by a ſmall pump kept for that purpoſe. This hand-pump muſt be ſo high as to throw the liquor into the copper; and by this means here is the whole matter of conveying the water into the maſh-tub, the wort into the receiver, and thence back again into the copper again, without the common troubleſome and waſteful method of ladling it by bowls from one veſſel to another.

There ſhould be two coolers, or backs as they are uſually called; and, to proportion them to a copper of a hogſhead, they ſhould be each ten feet long, and five feet wide in the clear, their depth very little. They ſhould be lined with milled lead as the

the receiver, and placed againſt the wall as near as may be to the copper, one at two feet from the ground, and the other two feet above that.

The working-veſſel or tun ſhould be placed at ſome ſmall diſtance from the coolers, and ſhould be of a ſquare ſhape, and lined throughout with the ſame milled lead as the others; and the whole ſhould be ſo diſpoſed, if poſſible, that the cellar may be near, and be ſo much lower than this working-tun, that the beer can be conveyed by a cock and a pipe out of that veſſel into the caſks.

Theſe ſhould be made ſo ſmooth on the inſide, that no fur or foulneſs can ſtick to them: but of this we ſhall treat hereafter. Our preſent buſineſs is in the brew-houſe; and it is neceſſary to underſtand this perfectly before we meddle with the affair of the cellar. There muſt be in the brew-houſe an oar to ſtir the malt in the maſh, bowls and other ſmall utenſils for examining the li-

C 6 quor,

quor, and a pipe lined with lead for conveying the liquor or wort from one of the veſſels to another. This pipe ſhould be made of ſolid good timber, and ſhould be five inches diameter in the clear. By this full ſize it will never waſte any of the liquor by ſtoppage; or by over-haſty pumping bubble out at the top, as pipes of ſmaller bore are very apt to do, when managed ever ſo little amiſs.

This is the compleat furniture of a brew-houſe. It may be contrived at leſs expence; but what is here ſet down will not be any great price; and, when the veſſels are once made in this manner, the buſineſs is done, not only for the owner's life, but for ſeveral generations. The common veſſels are frequently out of order: theſe which are lined with lead are ſubject to ſcarce any accidents. The beſt ſort of lead for doing them, is that of four pound to the foot; and every common work-

man

man will know how to manage the business.

Common tubs may serve in the place of these to those who dislike this expence; and even a part of these may perhaps be spared, according to the newest method of brewing, which is that of working the beer only in the cask. This will be the subject of a chapter in the succeeding part of this treatise.

CHAP. IX.

Of the several Operations in Brewing.

THE course of the malt-liquor in the common way of brewing is this: from the pump or cock the water is delivered to the copper; from thence it is let in to the mash-tub, when it is impregnated with the virtue and strength of the malt; thence it is let into the receiver, where it runs pure from the malt; and from this it is pumped into

into the copper again, in order to be the better impregnated with the hop. Thence it is again pumped out into the coolers, and from theſe it is conveyed into the working-tub; and, finally, from thence into the caſk, where it is to be kept.

This is the round of the liquor from pure water to malt-drink; and in theſe ſeveral veſſels the changes are gradually made.

The making of theſe changes, or the operations of brewing, ſhould be underſtood in general before we come to ſpeak of the abſolute practice. This is the way to be perfectly underſtood: and, for want of this, the common directions are uſeleſs; ſince, in giving an account of brewing, it is neceſſary to uſe the names of veſſels, and of the operations performed in them, which can never be underſtood unleſs thoſe articles are firſt explained.

CHAP.

CHAP. X.

Of Maſhing.

THE maſhing is the mixing and ſteeping the malt in the water, in order to obtain its virtue; and upon this depends the ſucceſs of all the ſucceeding operations. As the malt is ſo well prepared to give its virtue to the water, a moderate degree of heat is ſufficient for that purpoſe: but this ſhould, if poſſible, be preſerved for ſome time regularly, and that would prevent all the miſtakes of long maſhing, and of beating the malt, which we have ſhewn to be very wrong, and which always ſpoil the beer. We find by experience, that water, of a certain moderate degree of warmth alone, is fit to extract the virtue of malt; for, if it ſhould be put in cold, very little of its ſtrength would be obtained; and, if it ſhould be put on boiling

boiling hot, the conſequence would be the ſame; the malt would part with little of its ſtrength. This may ſeem very ſtrange; but it is equally true, and every common brewer knows it. Now, as one degree of heat alone does really take out the virtue of the malt, the perfection of maſhing would be to continue that degree of it. In the common way the malt is put into the water, when it is of this fit degree of heat, as well as the brewer can judge of it, and in general tolerably right; but from that moment it continues cooling. So that if the heat were ever ſo perfectly right at the time, it does not continue ſo to do any ſervice. This has occaſioned the beating of the malt in ſome places, and the over-long keeping it in the maſh in others: both of which are very wrong; the one thickening the liquor with abſolute flour, the other deadening it with the earthy part of the grain.

The

The perfection of mashing would therefore be, to keep the water and malt at that right degree of heat at which they were put together, for so long time as would serve for extracting all the valuable part of the malt, and no longer. This may be done by placing the mashing-tub in a larger vessel full of hot water, which may be replenished with fresh-heated water as it cools: the mash may thus be kept in one due degree of heat for the whole time. In this way two hours will extract the full virtue of the malt; and this will prove one of the greatest improvements in brewing.

This we shall direct hereafter with all particulars; but it will be first proper to explain the other operations, and give the common method of brewing.

CHAP.

CHAP. XI.

Of Hopping the Liquor.

THIS is the ſecond capital operation of brewing. When the maſh is finiſhed, the liquor impregnated with the ſtrength of the malt is let out into the receiver, ſtrained from the grains. The liquor is in this ſtate called wort: it is prepared for working, but there requires firſt of all to give it the flavour and the virtue of the hop. This is done in the common way, by a great deal of boiling. We have obſerved already, that a very little, with proper management, will anſwer the purpoſe, and the drink will be proportionably better. Therefore, in order to this, the hops ſhould be rub'd to pieces thoroughly between the hands, and then put in a bag into the receiver, for the wort to run gradually upon them. After

this

this gentle wetting and ſoaking, they will give their virtue with a few minutes boiling; and the drink will be not only better flavoured with this ingredient, but will be the better alſo in itſelf by ſparing the reſt of the boiling.

CHAP. XII.

Of Working the Beer.

WHEN the wort has been duly boiled with the hops, it is to be pumped into the coolers; and from thence, when cooled, it is to be let into the working-tun. It has now all the ſtrength of the malt, and the full virtue of the hop, and requires only fermentation in order to give it that ſpirit we expect in beer. The common way is to work it in a large open veſſel; but by that means a great deal of the ſpirit of the liquor is loſt; nor is there a due regard ſhewn to the neceſſary

neceſſary time, or to the degree of the fermentation. The regulating this degree of working will be one great article of the improvement of brewing; and the drink will be rendered much more ſpirituous, by covering up the working-tun very carefully. We ſhall have occaſion to ſhew in the ſucceeding chapters that a cloſer veſſel is much fitter for this purpoſe.

CHAP. XIII.

Of Brewing in general.

HAVING thus laid down the ſyſtem or theory of brewing, and explained the ingredients, the utenſils, and the ſeveral operations, we may ſafely proceed to the practiſe of the art; as every term will be underſtood, and all the neceſſary directions will appear plain and familiar.

We

We propoſe to treat of the making all the kinds of malt-liquors, of whatſoever denominations, and to direct all kinds of brewing. The moſt new and improved methods will be laid down in their place. But we ſhall begin with the old, directing the common way of family-brewing in a method ſomewhat more regular than it is uſually performed; and from thence proceeding to the neweſt improvements.

There are two great differences in all brewing, ariſing from the making ſtrong and ſmall together, or brewing each ſeparate. Of theſe two methods, the way of brewing each by itſelf is vaſtly the beſt; and we ſhall direct the particulars of it. But as many are fond of the old way, and think it eaſieſt and cheapeſt, we ſhall firſt give the beſt way of doing that. Upon this plan we are now to enter upon the practice of brewing, by directing the beſt

beſt method of making ſtrong and ſmall in the old way together.

In all methods of brewing there is a certain degree of fermentation neceſſary for impregnating the water with the full ſtrength of the malt; and many very diſagreeable ingredients have been uſed even by families to promote it: but theſe are not neceſſary. A due degree of heat being preſerved, a ſufficient care may in this reſpect be ſafely put in the place of all thoſe other materials that is needful, and nothing more. Too long maſhing we have ſhewn, is to be avoided; and a very little boiling of the hops is ſufficient; and this is what gives the general improvement in family-brewing. He will ſucceed beſt who can bring his malt ſooneſt to give out its virtue, and can impregnate the liquor in the eaſieſt and ſhorteſt way with the hop; for this delicate fruit looſes its very nature in tedious preparations.

The

The malt muſt be broke in order to its communicating its virtue freſh to the water; and that is done by a mill. It is not to be ground fine; for though many practiſe this, it is a great error. If it be only cracked, ſo that no grain comes out whole, it is ſufficient; for the intent is, that the water ſhould take out the virtue of the malt, not be mixed with it in the manner of paſte or gruel.

When the malt is ground, it ſhould lie ſometime to mellow in the air. This ſhould be in a cool room, where no ſun comes. The time it will require to lie is different, according to the kind. The brown malts ſhould be allowed three days; the pale kinds only two or one, for the quantity of fire uſed in drying the brown malts makes the air take effect upon them the more ſlowly. After this lying in the air, leſs maſhing anſwers the purpoſe: the ſtrength of the malt is more perfectly extracted; and the beer will be conſiderably

ſiderably ſtronger, than it would with the ſame quantity of malt any other way. The great care muſt be, that it gets no damp in lying. The place muſt be cool, and perfectly dry.

When the malt is ground, it will be time to look to the brewing-veſſels, for all poſſible care muſt be taken that they are ſound and clean. Cleanlineſs is as eſſential in the brew-houſe as in the dairy: fermentation, on which all depends, is a very nice article; and the leaſt mixture of foulneſs will diſturb the operation: the leaſt ill-ſcent in a veſſel will alſo communicate itſelf to the liquor.

Every tub, and every utenſil, ſhould be boiled in the copper, or very well ſcalded, then thoroughly ſtrained, and then ſcalded again, and after this expoſed to the air to ſweeten. This being done, while the malt lies to mellow, we may proceed to brewing.

The

The greater quantity of beer is brewed at a time, the better the work always ſucceeds: therefore it is adviſeable in families to brew as much at once as the brewing-veſſels will hold. But though this be always an advantage, the ſmalleſt family may brew for their own uſe with profit; and they will have their beer of every kind much better, purer, and wholeſomer than they can buy. The trouble is not great; and the ſaving is at leaſt one third part of the price, at the ſame time that the beer in every kind is better. To accommodate our directions to ſmall families, we ſhall conſider the brewing of only five buſhels of malt; which is to be done into ſtrong and ſmall beer in the follow-manner, and, with due care, will anſwer fully to expectation.

D CHAP.

CHAP. XIV.

The Practice of Brewing in ſmall Families.

A Copper that holds twelve pails of water, will anſwer very well for five buſhels of malt. Suit the water to the kind of malt, according to the directions in the preceding chapters; and, having filled the copper with it, make a briſk fire: when the water begins to be hot, ſprinkle upon the ſurface of it half a peck of the malt, without ſtirring it in. Let it ſwim upon the top till the water ſimmers, and juſt is beginning to boil: then draw, or ladle it out of the copper into the maſh-tub, and let it ſtand to cool a little. A thick ſteam riſes from it at firſt, and is ſcalding hot. This by degrees abates in quantity and heat; and when a man can hold his head over it, and look down upon the

the water, ſo as to ſee his face in it, then it will be in a proper condition for the malt. Save out half a buſhel, which will be wanted afterwards; and then pour the reſt gently into the maſh-tub, where the water is. While one perſon pours in the malt leiſurely and ſlowly, let another ſtir it all about in the water with the oar, and continue ſtirring it ſome time after all is in, that the whole may be very thoroughly and very well maſhed together. Some ignorant perſons beat the malt in the maſh-tub to break it, and force out the flour into the water; but this we have ſhewn is wrong. It ſhould be very well ſtirred in, that all parts of it may be wet; but nothing more. The beating it about in the maſhing brings it to the ſame caſe as if it had been ground too fine; which was what we have ſo carefully directed the brewer to avoid. The water is intended to take the tincture of the malt, not to be made into a maſs with the flour of it. When the whole is well ſtirred into the water, ſprinkle on the half buſhel of malt that was ſaved out, and then cover the maſh-tub with ſeveral ſacks laid one upon another, to keep in the heat; for the degree of warmth the water had when the maſh was made, muſt be kept up as carefully as poſſible.

When the tub is covered, let the copper be filled with water again, and bring it to boil with a briſk fire. This ſhould be ready about two hours after the maſh-tub is covered up: the ſacks are then to be taken off; and this boiling hot water out of the copper is to be let into the maſh in the tub. At the ſame time open the tap of the maſh-tub a very little way, ſo as to let out a ſtream about as thick as a crow-quill, to run into the receiver, or under back; and let the liquor run off in this manner, till there is as much come out as will fill the copper. This is

the

the prime wort, and has all the fine flavour of the malt; and it will be as clear as fine old beer. When this fine firſt wort is in the copper, tie up a pound and half of hops in a coarſe canvaſs bag, and put them into the copper to it. Theſe will ſwim upon the ſurface at firſt; but, during the boiling, they will ſink to the bottom; and this is the common rule taken that the boiling is ſufficient. But this is not certain; and there are other rules by which to know it. It is an article of the greateſt importance: for much leſs boiling will do than is commonly uſed: and if any more be allowed than is abſolutely neceſſary, the beer will certainly be the worſe for it.

The drier the hop is the ſooner it will ſink, and the greener it is the longer it will keep upon the ſurface. Experience ſhews this; and we find alſo, that when the hop ſinks quick, from its having been very dry when uſed, the virtue is not all

D 3 got

got out of it ſo ſoon as it goes to the bottom. Therefore though this be a good general hint, it will by no means anſwer for an exact rule: the eye will be a judge when the wort is boiled enough by its breaking; but the beſt judgment of all is laſtly to be found by the taſte.

Therefore, when the wort has boiled ſome little time, take up a little of it in a bowl, and let it ſtand in the cold ſome time; it will curdle, and ſeparate as it were, and this is called the breaking of the wort: a part of it will grow together into little lumps and be muddy; and, by continuing the boiling, theſe lumps will unite and ſink to the bottom, in one maſs. The liquor will be then clear again, and the boiling is by this judged to be ſufficient; but the taſte is alſo to be called in on this occaſion; and by this alone we can properly judge when the hop has given its full virtue to the wort, for that

that is the beſt of all rules to know when to give over the boiling.

The breaking is altered in point of time by ſo many accidents, that it is very difficult to judge by it with any degree of certainty. The larger the quantity of wort that is boiled, the ſooner it breaks. This is one obſervation that conſtantly holds. Then the older the malt, the ſooner alſo it breaks; for if the malt be taken freſh from the kiln, it will ſcarce give any breaking in the wort at all. Thirdly, the degree of fire brings it on ſooner or later; for always the quicker the wort boils, other circumſtances being equal, the ſooner it breaks: for the quickneſs of the motion encreaſes the tendency to it.

From all this it appears, that ſo many accidents may influence the breaking of the wort, that it cannot be admitted alone, for a certain rule to determine ſo nice a matter as the due boiling of the wort: and this is ſo eſſential, that all the reſt of the articles are of leſs importance. It has been the cuſtom in general, as we have obſerved, to allow too much boiling: and this, beſide deadening the taſte, really impoveriſhes the beer in ſtrength: for the ſediment is made of the mealy part of the malt, and the heavier tincture of the hop: it therefore contains a part of the ſtrength that was originally in the wort; and the longer the whole is boiled the more this ſediment will encreaſe; and therefore the more ſtrength will be loſt.

In fine, as to the breaking, it happens from theſe various cauſes, ſo uncertainly, that it will be ſeen ſometimes in a quarter of an hour, and ſometimes not in two hours; and therefore it can never be allowed a proper rule by which to manage the boiling. Neither is it any more neceſſary for the ſake of clearneſs in the beer; for it is eaſy to make beer without boiling at all, or with ſo little

little boiling, that the curdling ſhall not be ſeen, and yet that beer ſhall be as perfectly clear as any that can be brewed.

For theſe reaſons, by whatſoever rule the brewer is guided, he will find it an eſſential article not to let the wort boil too long; for the fineſt part of the malt, and the light pleaſant flavour of the hop, are evaporated by it, and the liquor is rendered weaker and more dead to the taſte. Therefore let him carefully attend to the ſeveral obſervations before laid down of the accidents that make the wort break ſooner or later; and, at the ſame time that he looks into the wort, let him alſo taſte it. He will thus find when the hop has given its beſt flavour; and let him not wait for the falling of more of the ſediment, but get it out at once into the tubs. It muſt then be drawn or ladled out of the copper, and run through a ſieve, that it may go clear into the coolers.

D 5 Then

Then this quantity is to ſtand to cool; and, in the mean time, the maſh in the tub may be ſtirred about with more warm water; and, if he pleaſes, ſtrengthened with a little freſh malt, as is the cuſtom of the London common brewers, and then drawn off and boiled up with the ſame quantity of hops; and in the ſame manner in all particulars.

This is the plain method of brewing, as far as the boiling off: but in the practice of it there is to be a different courſe obſerved, according as the deſign may be to brew only ſtrong beer, or both ſtrong and ſmall.

In the method here directed, if ſome freſh malt be added to the ſecond maſhing, the wort from this will be according to the quantity, nearly as ſtrong as the firſt; and there will be the two coppers of clean, pleaſant, and wholeſome ſtrong beer. Any one may by the ſame rules, only by altering the quantity of malt, make it ſtronger or weaker

as

as he pleaſes. The remainder in the tub will make but a poor kind of ſmall beer, by maſhing it again with cold water, and boiling this up with the old hops: but when good ſmall beer is intended to be made at the ſame time with the ale, the different management muſt be in the ſecond maſh. Whatever ſtrength is to be given to the ſmall beer, muſt plainly be taken from the ſtrong; but even in this caſe, when good ſmall beer is deſigned, the firſt maſh muſt run off clear for the ſtrong, and with all its virtue; only the ſecond copper of water muſt be poured on quick, and ſuffered to run off in a large ſtream. This wort of the ſecond maſh will be very much inferior to the firſt; but, being mixed with it in the coolers, they will make together a good drink; and there will remain ſtrength and virtue enough in the malt to afford tolerable ſmall beer. However, a very ſmall addition of freſh malt will give

D 6

it ſo much ſpirit, that no one who brews both together ſhould ever omit to give the ſmall beer intended for his own table that aſſiſtance. According to this rule, to make the better ſort of ſmall beer after the ſtrong, when the ſecond wort is drawn off, put in a copper of water upon the grains, and pour over it, lightly and carefully, half a buſhel of freſh malt. Cover it up; and then drawing off leiſurely, boil it up with half the quantity of hops that was allowed to the former; and from the ſame grains, in the ſame manner, there may be yet drawn another running of ſmall beer: but this laſt will be very poor.

When the wort of the firſt maſhing grows cool, it is time to begin fermenting it. Yeaſt is the proper ingredient for the purpoſe; and, according to the way in which this article is managed, the beer will be better or worſe, whatever care has been taken in the preceding operations

tions. If the brewing be in winter, the yeaſt muſt be put in while the wort is milk-warm; but if it be in ſummer, it may ſtand to be cold firſt. The way to do it is this: ſome yeaſt muſt be put into a large bowl, and a little of the wort juſt warm mixed with it. The yeaſt will ſwim at the top at firſt; but after ſome time, with a little aſſiſtance, it will blend itſelf with the wort, and begin the expected fermentation. It is then to be mixed with the wort drawn from the coolers into the working-tun. The fermentation will encreaſe from time to time, and the whole ſurface of the liquor will by degrees be covered with a fine pale-coloured curly head, not riſing into a light froth, nor into great looſe bliſters; for theſe are wrong appearances in the head, and are generally owing to putting in the yeaſt while the wort is too hot. Some degree of heat is neceſſary to promote the fermentation; but a very

very little is ſufficient. In ſummer the very temperature of the air is enough; and the wort therefore never anſwers ſo well in fermentation at that ſeaſon as when all the heat of the fire is abſolutely gone. In the colder months, as much of it is to remain in the liquor as will give the ſame temper as the perfectly cooled wort in ſummer, and nothing more.

A quart of thick and good yeaſt is a proper quantity for the hogſhead of ſuch wort, as we have directed to be made by the two maſhings.

If the wort does not come on properly in the working, ſift over the ſurface, from a very cloſe ſieve, a little of the fineſt wheat-flour. It muſt fall ſo regularly and neatly as to cover the whole ſurface of the wort, making a kind of artificial head; which, keeping in the air, will ſoon produce that natural one that was before expected.

If

If this does not anſwer, the fault is moſt probably in the temperature of the air, which ſuffers the liquor to be colder than is proper for fermentation. The beſt way to remedy this, is by encloſed hot water.

Fill a ſtone jugg with boiling water, and let it down gradually into the wort. It will ſink to the bottom of the veſſel, warming the liquor all the way it goes down; and, when at the bottom, will communicate a gentle glow to the whole; and, as the liquor warms, the fermentation will gradually and properly come on.

The common practice is to heat a little of the wort, and put it to the reſt: but this is a coarſe, irregular, and violent method; therefore it does not ſucceed ſo well: the other ſeldom fails.

There are other methods of encreaſing the fermentation, by the addition of particular ingredients; of which we ſhall ſpeak hereafter.

Ginger

Ginger is the uſual addition among the good houſewives; and the common brewers find a peculiar uſe in the purging root jalap. They uſe more of this drug than all the apothecaries in the kingdom. This is a truth the druggiſts will atteſt; and which the government, which has ſo lately and ſo eminently diſtinguiſhed itſelf by the care of bread, ſhould take into conſideration. If the eaſy methods before directed fail to raiſe the working to a proper pitch, a handful of bran tied up in a piece of canvaſs, and put into the fat, will often anſwer the deſign: or if this fail, the farther addition of two or three whites of eggs, beat up with brandy.

On the contrary, when beer works too violently, which is often the caſe, from too much yeaſt, too warm weather, or the like circumſtances, it will be checked at once, and brought to a right condition, by putting in a little freſh wort cold,

and

and ſtirring it gently about with a bowl. A little of the wort ſhould therefore be always reſerved for this purpoſe. If this does not ſucceed, rub a piece of clean oak board over with a ſmall bit of freſh butter, and lay this gently in at one ſide of the fat, taking it out as ſoon as it has been there long enough to ſhew its firſt effect.

When the fermentation is brought to a proper ſtandard or degree, the care muſt be to keep it at that for a due time. This ſhould not be leſs than two days and nights; and, if ſomewhat longer, the better.

It is a cuſtom in ſome places to beat the yeaſt into the working wort from time to time, and thus to keep it in the working-tun for a week or longer. The beer is rendered very ſtrong by this method; but it is neither ſo pleaſant as it will be when worked only a moderate time, nor ſo wholeſome. In the other way, which is the true practice, when the

the yeaſt begins to fall, put up the drink into the veſſel; and, when it has done working in the veſſel, it will be fit for ſervice. The ſmall beer is to be managed in the ſame way: and thus there will be a hogſhead of ale, and the ſame quantity of ſmall beer, of more or leſs ſtrength, according to the different management; and theſe will be pleaſant and wholeſome.

This may be called the common family way of brewing; and it will anſwer very well for the uſual method, where the perſon is not nice or delicate in his malt-liquor, nor intends it for keeping; but is content to brew as often as his caſk is out, and to drink the general run of home-brewed liquor.

But the practice of brewing is capable of being carried to a much greater perfection: and the firſt advance toward that is, to brew every kind of malt-liquor ſeparate. The ſeveral methods we ſhall now pro-

ceed

ceed to direct, according to the lateſt and beſt diſcoveries. And we may venture to ſay, that no art whatſoever has in late years been the ſubject of ſo many improvements as this of brewing.

Malt-liquors, when we ſpeak of them in general, are of three kinds, 1. STRONG BEER, which is intended for keeping, and is called October, becauſe the beſt is brewed in that month: 2. ALE, which is a ſtrong malt-liquor, but not deſigned for keeping: and, 3. SMALL BEER, which, when made but of a moderate ſtrength in the way we ſhall direct, will keep a very conſiderable time, and be improving all the while.

CHAP.

C H A P. XV.

The Method of Brewing the fineſt Strong Beer.

IF the conveniences of the brewhouſe will ſerve for brewing three or four hogſheads of October or ſtrong beer at a time, that will be the beſt practice. We will ſuppoſe three hogſheads. The receipt will equally ſerve for any larger or ſmaller quantity, only allowing the due proportion of the ingredients. For brewing the three hogſheads, chuſe five quarters of fine ſweet malt. Let it be ſuch as has been malted about a quarter of a year, and has lain in a large heap all that time to mellow. See that it be perfectly ſound, fine, tender, and entirely clean from duſt or any other mixture. Let this be ground with care, juſt ſo much, that every grain is fairly broken, and no more: then lay it up in a heap in a cool

cool ſhady place, and let it lie eighteen hours. Thus will you have a perfect fine malt, in the exact right condition for brewing.

CHAP. XVI.

Of Maſhing.

CHUSE a ſweet, clean and well-taſted water, ſofter or harder according to the nature and kind of the malt, but perfectly pure. When the water is got into the copper, put in a quarter of a pound of hops with it, and an ounce of common ſalt; and, when it begins to heat, ſift over it, through a coarſe ſieve, as much malt as will juſt coat it over to keep in the ſpirit. When this is on, briſk up the fire, and bring the water to ſimmer; but don't let it boil up: then draw it off at once into the maſh-tub, which muſt be placed in a larger tub, as before obſerved, with the coat of malt upon it; and let

let it ſtand till the thick vapour ceaſes, and you can conveniently look down into it, and ſee your face. When it is in this condition, pour in the malt, a little at a time, and let ſome other perſon ſtir it about all the while it is running in, that there may be no clodding of it together in any part. When all is in, let the ſtirring be continued a little, that you may be ſure every part of the malt is free and well-mixed with the liquor: then fill up the cavity between the outſide of the maſh-tub and the outer veſſel with water of the ſame heat, that in the maſh-tub was when the malt was put in: keep water boiling to ſupply the place of this as it cools: obſerve the temper of it at firſt, and once in ten minutes draw off as much of that which is cool as will be needful to make room for ſo much freſh boiling water as will bring the whole to the ſame heat it had at firſt; and every time the freſh

fresh hot water is put into the space between the two vessels, give a very slow and gentle stirring to the malt in the mash-tub.

In these double vessels there is to be always one cock that communicates with the space between the two where the water is to let that out as it cools, and another through the real bottom and false bottom of the mash-tub, which goes also thro' the outer vessel, for discharging the clear wort, when the mashing is done, into the receiver. No mashing-vessel of any other kind can keep a due heat, or answer the purpose of opening the substance of the malt; for if the water be too hot when the malt is put in, it hardens instead of dissolving it; and if it be too cool at first, it soon grows into full condition of service. The malt is to be kept in the mash-tub in this manner one hour and three quarters; and in that time another copper of water, equal to the first, must

muſt be made ready, covering it with a head of malt, and bringing it juſt to ſimmer.

A little before this ſecond copper of water is ready, the firſt wort is to be begun to be run off; and the hops are to be prepared for ſoaking in it as it runs. This is the improved method of brewing. The whole quantity of hops for the three hogſheads of this beer, which is intended for keeping a conſiderable time before it is uſed, muſt be eighteen pounds, that is, ſix to each hogſhead. Therefore, as the quantity of one hogſhead is now in the maſh, take ſix pound of hops, ſprinkle them over with a very little ſalt, and rub them well to pieces between the hands. Tie them up in a looſe bag of coarſe canvaſs, and put them into the receiver, that is, under the maſh-tub: then let the wort run clear out at the tap in the maſh-tub in a ſmall ſtream, not thicker than a large ſtraw; and let it it run upon theſe bruiſed hops. This will ſoak them, ſo that they will readily, and at once as it were, give their full virtue, when the wort comes to be boiled. The ſalt that is put to the water, and to the hops, is not enough to give the leaſt taſte to the wort; but it will give it a kind of ſpirit that water alone never has; and will make it extract, much better than it otherwiſe would, the virtues both of the malt and of the hops.

As the wort drains from the malt in the maſh-tub, there muſt be a gradual ſupply from the copper of boiling water. The intent is, that a hogſhead of wort be run off; but though ſomething more than a hogſhead of water was uſed, to allow for the quantity that the malt ſoaks up without return; yet this whole quantity muſt not be had from what was firſt in the maſh-tub. There are to be three ſuch maſhings from this quantity of the malt; and one

E is

is to follow another without letting the malt ever grow dry. Therefore, when the liquor is ſo far drained out of the maſh-tub, that the malt begins to look dry, let ſome of the hot water be let out of the copper into the maſh-tub; and ſtir the malt well about in it. This muſt be let in very gradually, cooling it firſt to a due degree; and by this means there is to be a ſupply of water kept to the malt, while the firſt wort runs off: ſo that when there is a copper full run into the receiver, the ſecond copper of water will be all got into the maſh-tub.

The hops will have been all this time ſoaking; and the copper being now empty, the wort in the receiver muſt be pumped or ladled into it, and the hops put in with it; then the fire muſt be made up, and the wort muſt be brought to boil briſkly. Let it boil a quarter of an hour, and no longer: then let it be drawn off into the cooling backs; and the

copper

copper be filled the third and laſt time with water.

In this proceed exactly as before. The ſecond copper is now maſhing; it muſt be ſtirred gently about, and there muſt be boiling water from time to time added as before to the quantity, between the maſh-tub and the outer veſſel, to keep up an equal degree of heat. This maſhing muſt laſt an hour and three quarters; and in that time the third copper of water muſt be got to a due degree of heat.

When the time is near expired, ſix pounds more of the hops muſt be juſt ſprinkled over with a tea-ſpoonful of ſalt, and thoroughly rubbed to pieces in the hands again: then they muſt be tied up in a bag as the former, and put into the receiver. The ſecond maſh having now been kept at a due degree of heat, the appointed time the wort is to be let out in a ſmall ſtream into the receiver, running upon the hops. Manage this exactly as before; and, when ſo much of the wort has run off that the malt begins to be dry, let in ſome of the water again out of the copper. This may be of a degree of heat, ſomewhat greater than the firſt or ſecond; becauſe the grains having already parted with a great deal of their ſtrength, require it, and becauſe being to be maſhed a laſt time, ſomething more in point of heat is neceſſary.

When there is the full quantity of a hogſhead run out of this ſecond wort, ſtop the cock of the maſh-tub, let in the remainder of the water from the copper, and immediately put in the wort out of the receiver into the copper, with the bag of hops along with it.

A quantity of malt having been ſaved out for the purpoſes of covering the water and capping the maſh; both theſe articles muſt be duly attended to, in the three ſeveral operations we have thought it therefore

fore beſt, for the ſake of avoiding three repetitions, to name theſe articles here together. The quantity of water in each copper, is to be ſo much as will allow a full hogſhead of wort, beſide what the malt ſoaks up. Upon each copper full of water: there is to be ſpread a thin coat of malt to keep in the ſpirit; and over each maſh there is alſo to be ſpread the quantity of half a buſhel, by way of cap to the whole.

The third copper of water being now in the tub, and therefore the laſt maſh made, put on the cap of freſh malt, which is all that was left, and let it ſtand; keeping the water between the outer tub and the maſh-tub always of a due heat, to keep up the full degree of warmth in the maſh.

A ſmall copper will be neceſſary for the heating the water for this ſervice; becauſe the other will be conſtantly employed in the heating

E 3 the

the water, or boiling off the wort, the whole time of the brewing.

The ſecond running of wort being now in the copper, briſk up the fire, and bring it to boil: let it boil twenty-five minutes, and no longer; and then run this off into the coolers.

The buſineſs now becomes eaſy; there is only one maſhing remains, which is to be in the maſh-tub an hour and half, and no longer. Then rub the laſt quantity of hops, which is to be alſo ſix pounds, between the hands, without any ſalt; for the wort is now thinner, and will take effect upon them alone; tie them up in a bag, and put them into the receiver. When the maſh has ſtood its time, turn the cock to run a ſomewhat larger ſtream; and, when the liquor is all come off, pump it, or ladle it into the copper, and put in not only the hops new ſoaked, but alſo the two former parcels. Boil all together the ſame time that the laſt

laſt copper was boiled, and then let the wort run off into the coolers.

CHAP. XVII.

The Cooling.

THESE three worts being mixed, make one regular and excellent quantity, in which there is all the ſtrength and virtue of the malt very perfectly; and the entire flavour, and due bitter of the hops; without any of the earthy and heavy part of the grain, or of that auſtere and unpleaſant taſte which hops yield when they have undergone a vaſt deal of boiling.

The proof of this is eaſily found; for this beer will keep ever ſo long: and hence it is plain, that the hop has given all that was expected or required of it, a fine flavour, and a power of keeping: and as to the other, the fact is ſo evident, that the

E 4 wort

wort has all the virtue of the malt, that the grains are mere chaff.

If this brewing has been managed exactly according to the orders here laid down, there could not be ſmall beer made of the grains that any one could drink, the full virtue having been taken out by theſe repeated maſhings, with a continued heat.

If any one diſlikes the addition of this ſmall quantity of ſalt, it may be left out; but the beer will neither be ſo ſtrong, ſo briſk, nor ſo clear without it. As to the uſe of the double veſſel for maſhing, with the hot water between, that is eſſential. It is on this depends the entire virtue of the malt being taken into the wort.

One great advantage of the putting the hops into the receiver is, that the beer which is made thus never foxes, as the brewers call it: but the great article is, that being thus ſoaked by degrees, and ſteeped in the

the water, they will give out their virtue with ſo little boiling, as will not damage the drink; for when the wort is boiled too long, as is the moſt common of all errors in brewing, it becomes too thick to ferment perfectly, and its ſediment can never get clear down; ſo that all the pains which can be beſtowed, and all the judgment that can be employed afterwards, will never make it good and perfectly fine drink.

One thing there is in this receipt which differs from the common practice, and the uſual opinions: this is the degree of boiling given to the three coppers of worts. It is cuſtomary to boil the ſecond longer than the firſt, and the third longer than the ſecond; and, with the common way of making, this is certainly right: but when the malt is kept up in its proper heat all the time, by the water between the two tubs, leſs and leſs boiling always anſwers for the ſucceeding worts. The time here directed for each, is nearly what does, and perhaps comes as cloſe to a good general rule, as any meaſure of time can; nay, we may add, if the malt be juſt ſuch as is directed, and the whole managed regularly from the beginning, this very time almoſt to a minute will do the buſineſs; but the eye and taſte are the true and certain judges, and they muſt determine whether the worts ſhall be kept in the copper a few minutes longer, or run off a little ſooner than has been here directed.

C H A P. XVIII.

The Working.

THE worts in common brewing are uſually cooled ſeparate, and let down into the tun one after the other: but this is an injudicious practice; for the buſineſs is to mix them perfectly, without which they will not enter upon the great article of of fermentation regularly; and they can never be mixed ſo well as while the ſeveral parcels are all warm. 'Tis therefore we have directed the running off the worts from the copper into the coolers, one to the other. And when there are two backs or coolers, as we have directed, that are large enough, the beſt way of all is this: let all the three worts run into the upper of the two backs or coolers; and, when the third is in, let the whole ſtand two hours; then draw it off ſlowly and leiſurely into the under cooler or back, and by this means leave behind any coarſe ſediment that may have come in with it.

In this ſecond cooler let the whole ſtand till it is perfectly cold, if the weather be mild: but if the ſeaſon be very cold, let there be a very ſmall degree of heat remain in the wort: then draw it off leiſurely and ſlowly into the working-tun, ſo as not to diſturb the liqour in falling in, and to leave a ſecond ſediment in the cooler.

As in ſeveral points this receipt differs from the common practice, and from what are called the beſt receipts for this kind of beer, it may be neceſſary, as we go on, to ſay in what the difference conſiſts; that thoſe who chuſe the old way may follow it, and ſuch as prefer this, which is indeed vaſtly preferable, may underſtand the reaſons of the difference. The ſeveral points in which the variation conſiſts, may ſeem little; but it is on theſe little things the excellence of brewing depends.

It is a common direction that the worts is to lie thin for cooling; and the uſual practice, which in theſe caſes is to let the worts, one parcel after another, into the coolers, and thence into the tun, favours it; but experience in this perfect method of brewing ſhews otherwiſe. In this way the whole three hogſheads of wort are to be in the upper cooler together;

gether; and this way the whole will cool more ſlowly indeed, but much better, than in the three parcels; for while it cools in this large body, it mellows all the time, and it loſes leſs of the ſpirit; for when the wort is laid thin, as brewers expreſs it, that is, a ſmall quantity in a broad cooler, the air has great power in evaporation; and the wort not only becomes thicker, by what it loſes in the cooling; but what is much more eſſential even than that, this loſs is of the moſt ſpirituous and excellent part.

Theſe are the diſadvantages attending the common practice, and the common rules for ſpreading the wort thin: but beſides the benefit ariſing from the preventing theſe by our method of cooling in a large body, there are ſeveral particular advantages attending this practice. The mellowing of the wort from a perfect mixture of its parts is one; another is the certainty that all the three

three runnings are perfectly mixed one with the other; and conſequently, every part of the liquor is alike before the working begins: and thirdly, the dropping ſome coarſe matter twice over, namely, once in each cooler, which being the heavieſt part of the ingredients, and, perhaps, ſome accidental foulneſs with it, would have prevented the regular and perfect fermentation. Every one knows how delicate and nice a point the working of beer is, and how ſmall a quantity of any improper ſubſtance is able to check it: therefore this is a very uſeful practice which gives any ſuch matter, that may by accident have got in, time to ſeparate from the wort. The perfect mixing of the ſeveral parcels of wort, is a point as eſſential to the regular fermentation, though it be not ſo well underſtood, for the working never begins regularly, unleſs it begins in the whole liquor at a time; and it never can do that, unleſs the ſeveral

ſeveral portions of it are perfectly mixed. This mixture cannot be ſo well made in the common way of brewing; but in this method it is done compleatly, partly by the time the three parcels ſtand together in the upper cooler, partly by the running of the whole from the upper to the under; and, finally, by the running of the whole in that cool and eaſy manner into the working-tun.

Having now got the wort into the tun, and explained the reaſons of our particular practice in every article, we are to proceed to the fermenting or working of it. We have a fine ſubject to work upon; for this will be a clear, ſtrong, and excellent wort; and nothing is wanted but care to make this fermentation as compleat, in its kind, as any of the other operations.

When the wort is in the tun, immediately get to work upon the yeaſt. Care muſt be taken to get that which

is

is perfectly good, and it muſt be mixed with a little of the wort firſt, in a large bowl. Some of the wort muſt be ſaved for this purpoſe, as it is running into the tun, and a little more than is directly wanted for this ſervice; becauſe if the fermentation runs too high, which is what no body can foreſee whether it will or not, then a little of the cold unfermented wort is of all things the mildeſt and quickeſt method to check it.

The yeaſt muſt be thick, and in perfect good condition; and about three quarts will be ſufficient for the working this quantity of beer. It muſt be mixed very gradually with a ſmall quantity of wort let into the bowl for that purpoſe, and then the wort and yeaſt together gently into the tun. Cover it up cloſe, and watch it from time to time carefully, to ſee that the fermentation goes on as it ſhould. It ought to begin very gently, and encreaſe gradually;

dually; and if it proceed in this right manner, there will be first a smiling flowry head upon the whole liquor, and by degrees this will thicken into a yellowish white crust; and, upon holding the head a little over it, when uncovered, there will be a sharp penetrating scent arise. The head will from this time thicken more and more, and the scent will become more penetrating, for the space of three days and nights: at the end of this time it will naturally abate, and by degrees cease; and the drink is then to be got into the casks.

CHAP. XIX.

Of assisting a weak Fermentation.

THIS is the course of fermentation, when all goes as it should do; and to this we are to endeavour to bring the working, as nearly as we can, when, from unfavourable

vourable ſeaſons, or any other accidents, it does not go on naturally right.

According to the variety of theſe accidents, the fermentation will ſometimes be too ſlack, and ſometimes in the contrary extreme, too violent: theſe, as they ariſe from contrary cauſes, require perfectly different remedies: but of theſe the mildeſt are always beſt.

If the working does not come on ſufficiently, ſtir in the yeaſt with a clean whiſk lightly and gently, two or three times. This will bring it, in moſt caſes, to a juſt degree of fermentation. The whiſk muſt be made of a few long twigs, and it muſt be perfectly clean; then ſcald it in boiling water, and ſhake and wipe it dry with a clean cloth: this will preſerve ſome ſlight warmth, which, when it is uſed, will put the parts of the liquor it touches into a ſtate of gentle fermentation; and this, aſſiſted by the motion, and by the bring-

ing

ing in of the head, will extend itſelf to the whole. The whiſk muſt be uſed with a gentle and careful hand. The great point is to take it in time, for the mildeſt methods are always beſt; and theſe will do then, though they would not afterwards. The uſe of the whiſk alone, at a proper time, when the fermentation firſt ſlackens, will ſave the diſagreeable neceſſity of having recourſe to other expedients, all violent aſſiſtances being hurtful to the drink in the end; and many of thoſe which the common brewers uſe on this occaſion, being prejudicial to the health.

If by neglect, or any other accident, the wort in the working-tun be in ſuch a ſtate of low fermentation, that this mixing and ſtirring in the yeaſt will not bring it to be right, the expedients already mentioned, under the head of common brewing, are to be uſed. The ſifting a little fine flour over the ſurface, ſhould be the firſt tried; and the next ſhould

ſhould be the putting in a ſtone-bottle full of boiling hot water, covered cloſe down, that none of the water can poſſibly get out of the bottle to mix among the wort. If theſe are not ſufficient, the putting in a ſmall bag of bran is to be tried next. The practice of beating up whites of eggs with brandy, and putting them into the veſſel, is not ſo proper for theſe fine beers. But if good management be uſed, one or other of the methods here directed will bring the fermentation to a due height; or, if they fail ſingly, they may be uſed two or more together; always obſerving the rules of moderation, and being careful to avoid putting the wort into the other extreme, of too violent a fermentation; which is certainly as dangerous a fault at leaſt as the other. Thus, if whipping in the head alone, which is the way that always ſhould be tried firſt, does not ſucceed, put in the ſtone-bottle of hot water, and

whip

whip it in again from time to time as it riſes, with this aſſiſtance. In moſt caſes this will do: but, if it does not anſwer ſufficiently, put in ſuch another bottle of hot water well faſtened down, ſift over the wort a little creamy head of flour, and put in a ſmallbag of bran: then obſerve from time to time to whip in the yeaſt that riſes, and the working will ſoon be at its proper height.

Cloſer covering in all theſe caſes brings on the fermentation the more haſtily; and therefore, when there is occaſion to uſe ſeveral of theſe aſſiſtances together, becauſe of the difficulty of bringing it to work well, the covering ſhould always be increaſed in proportion; and ſhould not only lie cloſe over the top of the maſh-tub, but hang over the ſides down to the bottom.

CHAP.

CHAP. XX.

Of lowering a too violent Fermentation.

BY theſe means the wort may be brought to a regular way of working, when it is naturally ſlow: but there is equal care to be taken that it does not come on in too violent a degree; and on the appearance of this as much management is to be uſed to prevent it. Too much heat in the weather will ſometimes occaſion this exceſs of fermentation; and ſometimes, when a better ſeaſon is choſe, the ſame thing will follow from the yeaſt having been put in while there was too much heat in the wort. Theſe are the moſt uſual and the moſt obvious cauſes; therefore timely care ſhould be taken to avoid theſe accidents by a choice of cool weather, and by ſeeing that the wort is perfectly cooled in

I any

any thing warmer weather before it is put into the working-tub.

But if, from neglect of these cautions, or from any other cause, the wort ferments too furiously, if the head grows up too quick, rises too high, and swells up into large blisters: when this is seen in time, there is no great danger of harm arising from it; for as some of the wort has been saved out, and kept perfectly cold for this purpose, no more is needed than to put this to the rest. The whole or a part of it must be used according as the violence of the fermentation is greater or less; and this will seldom fail to check the fury of the working, and bring the whole to a due temper. The effect of this must be assisted by taking off the coverings from the working-tub, either in part or entirely: but when all is set right, and the degree of fermentation is what it should be, the tub must be covered up as close again as ever; for

for the more the ſpirituous vapour which riſes in fermentation is at liberty, the greater quantity always then riſes of it; and this being loſt is all ſo much loſs to the beer. But there is another reaſon why all poſſible care ſhould be taken to prevent too great a waſte of this, which is, that a ſecond fermentation of the beer, though of a lighter kind, muſt be expected when it is in the caſk. Without this it will never be fine; and this will not come on well if the ſpirit of the liquor has been waſted by this open working. It is for this reaſon, that beers which have been worked in an open working-tun, as ſome will do, always fail of that perfect clearneſs, and ſpirited taſte which thoſe have which have been worked under care. And for this reaſon no beers are ſo perfectly fine and briſk, as thoſe which have been worked only in the caſk, when that has been well-managed, and has ſucceeded happily. This is

a me-a method of which we ſhall ſpeak in a ſucceeding chapter, and care and perfect right management may make it very ſucceſsful: however, no method can exceed this which we are here giving, when it is managed right in all articles.

If the putting in of the cold raw wort, and uncovering the working-tub for a time does not anſwer the expectation in checking the violence of the fermentation, let no ingredients of any kind be added; but open the door and windows, and let in a freſh and thorough air. If this does not check it, draw out the wort out of the tub into four or five ſmaller veſſels, and let it lie as ſhallow in them as is neceſſary. This will abate at pleaſure the exceſs of the head; and it is not only a certain remedy in caſe of extremities, but is eaſily proportioned to the degree of the exceſs. Thus, when the working is very furious, a greater number of veſſels may be uſed for

F drawing

drawing it into, that it may lie very thin; and, when it is not ſo violent, a ſmaller number may ſerve. The common practice is to put in a parcel of pewter plates and diſhes: theſe operate by the greaſe which remains upon them notwithſtanding waſhing; and a cleanlier method is the buttered board directed for this purpoſe in common brewing: but neither is proper. When the fermentation is well regulated, it is to continue about the time we have named, that is, two days and a half, or at the moſt three: but in this caſe nature is to determine; for it is not the number of hours, but the condition of the wort, that is to aſcertain the time of putting it into the caſk. In this caſe no arts are to be uſed to prolong the fermentation, but at a natural time when it begins to ceaſe the liquor is to be got into the barrels. If the yeaſty head be beat down as it riſes, the wort may be kept fermenting eight or nine

nine days; and the drink would be the ſtronger for this: but it would be ill-taſted, and never perfectly fine, without worſe arts than thoſe here uſed to make it ſo. The intent in this brewing, which is meant for the fineſt beer, is, that the fermentation ſhould riſe naturally to its proper height, and in the ſame manner ſhould take its natural decline. The ſpirit is to be kept in by covering the wort while working, and this will naturally continue the working perhaps ten or twelve hours longer than it would have been if open; then the head will begin to fall, the ſharp vapour from the wort will riſe in a leſs degree, and every thing will be plainly coming to a ſtate of reſt. This is the time for getting the wort into the caſk, for it is intended to take a ſecond fermentation there. The motion of the liquor in getting it into the veſſel will contribute to this; but it will not come on well,

F 2 unleſs

unleſs there be ſome power of the firſt fermentation left there to bring it on. Art may anſwer the purpoſe of bringing on a fermentation in the caſk, when the original working is entirely over; but that is not the purpoſe: nor will the liquor ever be perfect if managed in this manner. The fermentation in the caſk ſhould be a continuation of that in the tun, not a new one brought on after the other was over; and it is this, and this only, which can make the drink perfectly fine and clear.

CHAP. XXI.

Of Caſking the Beer.

THEREFORE, when the falling of the head ſhews the fermentation to be declining, let the wort be let out of the tun. This muſt be done by a cock, and that ſhould be let into the tun at five inches above the bottom, for ſo much will be thick, making

making a kind of ſediment; and this muſt be carefully left behind: only the pure and clear wort being taken off. This ſediment is not altogether uſeleſs, tho' it muſt not be let into the caſk of the fine beer; it is conſiderably ſtrong, and will be a good addition to ſmall beer, which may be brewed after this, and while it is working. This is a point that has been diſputed; but there is no guide like experience, and that declares in favour of this way of uſing the large ſediment that is thus made from the drawing of the fine wort from the tun.

The caſks ſhould be got in perfect good order by the time the wort will be fit for puting into them; and this is eaſily done, becauſe we know perfectly when they will be wanted. Every thing ſhould be of the beſt kind for this excellent ſort of drink, and conſequently the caſks for keeping it ſhould be of good ſtuff, and well made. No wood is proper but heart of oak: and they ſhould be ſo well made, that the inſide being true and ſmooth, no foulneſs can lodge. If they have been painted ſome time, they will keep the drink the better, for the paint ſtops up the pores moſt perfectly, and by that means confines the ſpirit of the drink much better than plain wood: but this ought to be done in time, and they muſt be very well freed of ſcent, by ſtanding in the air, before they are uſed; for the abominable ſmell of freſh paint would certainly affect the beer while it was in ſo delicate a ſtate as working. Never put this fine beer into a new caſk: the true way to prepare the veſſels for it, is to ſcald them very well, over and over, and then keep one or two brewings of good ſmall beer in them. Theſe will thoroughly ſeaſon the caſk; and after this nothing will be required, but ſuch through good cleaning as may be given by boiling water, and a little hard broom. When caſks are paint-

ed,

ed, this ſhould be at the time of their firſt ſeaſoning, that, if any flavour of the paint ſhould be troubleſome, it may be in the ſmall beer, and not in ſuch as is of this value.

While the beer is put into the caſks, make a reſerve of ſome of it in a ſmall veſſel by itſelf, to fill up the others as they work over. It is a common practice to fill them up with the very beer that has worked out of the veſſel : but this is a coarſe method, and not fit to be uſed for theſe fine kinds of drink.

Let the beer be drawn ſoftly and carefully out of the working-tun, not to diſturb the ſediment it has made, and fill up the caſks quite full. The drawing from the tun to the caſk will put the whole in motion ; this will affect the languid fermentation; and the working will begin again. They muſt be ſuffered to work out at the bung-hole ; and, as the quantity is diminiſhed, that way make it up out of what was re-

F 4 ſerved

ſerved in the ſmall caſk for that purpoſe. This muſt be done with great care, not to diſturb the fermentation that is now going on in the liquor; and the beſt method of putting it in is by means of a tin-funnel, with a long ſpout: this ſhould be put in ſo far, that the end of the ſpout is two inches and a half buried in the beer, and then the liquor from the reſerved caſk muſt be gradually let into it, by pouring gently into the funnel. This will fill up the veſſel without giving the leaſt diſturbance to the liquor: and thus it ſhould be kept filling up from time to time during the working.

In this manner wait with patience the natural period of this ſlight fermentation: according to the nature of the malt, the water, the degree of boiling, or the ſeaſon of the year, but moſt of all according to the management of it in the working tun, this will be longer or ſhorter: ſo that no time can be

fixed

fixed when it ſhall be over: but when it is, and all is quiet, ſtop up the caſks cloſe, and let them ſtand till the beginning of the next year; that is, ſuppoſing the beer was brewed in October, which is in general the beſt time of all, it ſhould ſtand perfectly quiet, and without any mixture, till the following ſpring. In this time it will perfectly fine itſelf.

The cold of the winter ſtopping all inteſtine motion in the beer will aſſiſt in this; but in the begining of ſpring, the weather will take effect, and there will begin a new fermentation, which will laſt all ſummer. To prepare for this, the vent-hole muſt be opened, and it will be eaſy to ſee whether the fermentation is or is not begun. If it be, the vent-hole muſt be left open; and in that manner it is to continue all the ſummer; if the fermentation is not yet begun, the hole muſt be ſtopp'd again; and once in a week it muſt be opened to watch the beginning of this new fermentation.

This is a good time for putting in thoſe ingredients into the beer, which are ſometimes wanted: but we need not name them farther here; for in beer thus brewed, and managed throughout with this due care, there will be no occaſion for any aſſiſtance more than the beer will get itſelf from time. If the examination of the beer ſhould be omitted, till the fermentation had got any power, and the veſſel all this while pegg'd faſt down, there would be danger of its burſting; for tho' a very little communication with the air be ſufficient, as we ſee by opening the vent-hole; yet if the veſſel were every way cloſe, the power of the fermenting liquor would certainly deſtroy it.

The veſſel ſhould ſtand with this opening till autumn. Uſually a week before Michaelmas, or there-about, is the time when this laſt fomentation natu-

naturally ceafes: it was brought on by the encreafing heat of the air in fpring, and it goes off as it cools in autumn.

The beer may now be confidered as compleatly fermented: the hop will be mellowed in it, and one uniform tafte will prevail in the whole, which will be a mixture of the malt and hop mellowing one another; and neither will be predominant: therefore all this beer can poffibly want now, is perfect clearnefs. This is fo great a recommendation to all malt-liquor, that fuch as has been brewed with this expence and care, certainly fhould not be deficient in it. If it were now ftopp'd up, and to ftand the winter in quiet, it would of itfelf fine down, by fettling a fmall fediment, and be very clear: but it is eafy to help nature in this operation, and to caufe the fediment to fall more fully and more regularly. The only ingredient that need be ufed is ifinglafs; and this is fo perfectly innocent, that there is no need to decline its aſſiſtance. The beſt way of uſing it is thus.

Buy two ounces of beaten iſinglaſs; and take care that it is ſo well beaten, that there is no part of it thicker than a piece of thin paper: cut this very ſmall, draw out a gallon of the beer, and put this iſinglaſs to it; ſtir it well about from time to time, and let it ſtand till it is perfectly diſolved, then ſtrain the ſolution thro' a coarſe and perfectly clean cloth; take out the bung of the veſſel, and carefully put it in: ſtir this about to mix it with the whole, and then lightly lay over the bung: there will be ſome ſmall motion in the liquor from this, and the bung muſt not be put faſt down till it is over. Then faſten the bung, and only leave a little opening at the vent-hole: then let it ſtand three weeks, and it will then be perfect. It may either be drank from the caſk or bottled, and will be very fine, ſtrong, mellow, well taſted, and wholeſome. Where the intent is to drink it from

from the caſk, ſtill there ſhould be a reſerve of bottling, and the beſt way is to drink off two thirds by draught, and then bottle the reſt, which in a good cellar will ſoon be in excellent condition.

If the whole be intended to be bottled off, the time is at one year's end; in the ſame manner as for drinking from the caſk. If the beer be brew'd in October, it will be ready for bottling the October following; and, to give it full perfection, it ſhould ſtand a year in the bottles; ſo that the beginning of drinking it ſhould be two years old from the brewing.

This is the compleat method of brewing the October, or fine beer; and whoever will obſerve the ſeveral rules cannot fail of ſucceſs. As to the degree of ſtrength, what is here directed for the quantity of malt, will make ſuch as ſhall be ſufficiently potent; but it may be varied in this matter, at the pleaſure of the perſon, by encreaſing or diminiſhing the

the quantity of malt. The allowance in this receipt is about thirteen buſhels to the hogſhead. There are ſome who brew with only ten or eleven buſhels for this kind of drink; and others who go as far as twenty buſhels: but this ſeems to be a kind of medium between the ſtronger and the weaker kinds; what we call the ſtrong October being generally brewed with ſixteen buſhels to the hogſhead, for thoſe with twenty are too heady. There is no drink pleaſanter than this kind, with the degree of ſtrength here directed: and none can be more wholeſome.

CHAP. XXII.

Of Brewing common Family-Ale.

THE Liquor call'd ALE, in diſtinction from beer, is uſually of leſs ſtrength; and is leſs tinctured with the hop: being intended for drinking ſoon after it is brewed,

brewed; not for keeping years as the other. This ſhould be brewed alone, that is, without any ſmall-beer to be made from the ſame malt. The method of brewing is in general the ſame in all kinds; but as there are particulars needful to be regarded, in order to ſuit the operation to each particular kind of drink, we ſhall here give the method of brewing this kind, with all the needful management. With regard to the ſtrength, that is to be according to every one's particular pleaſure; but ſome ſtandard muſt be fixed for the directions to be given here; and therefore we ſhall make the allowance eight buſhels to the hogſhead; which will make a very excellent drink of this kind.

The beſt method is to mix it; and the proportion I have found moſt agreeable is ſix buſhels and a half of the amber malt, and one and a half of the high dried or brown; not the porter-malt, for that does not mix well

well in the maſh with any other; but any of the common high-dry'd malts.

Let this be ground together, and let it be made ſomewhat finer than the former kind; but ſtill not any thing like fine: every grain ſhould be broke and ſplit, that is, broke twice. The brewer will know by this what to direct; it cannot be done with any ſuch exactneſs; but this is a kind of ſtandard that may do by way of rule. Let this malt, when ground, ſtand in the ſack one day and night, or a few hours leſs than that; and then it will be fit for brewing. Chuſe for the water ſuch as is ſoft, no matter how it is in other reſpects. As much of this muſt be boiled as will allow for the ſoaking up of the malt, and afford a clear hogſhead of the wort, with allowance alſo for waſte. Set this on in the copper, put in a table-ſpoonful of ſalt, and make the fire briſk, a ſlight ſcum will riſe to the ſurface; take that off, and then ſprinkle on about three quarts of bran: let it remain

remain till the water ſimmer and is going to boil, then ſkim this alſo off, and the water will be perfectly clear and ready; damp the fire, and draw off half of the water into the maſh-tub; then let it ſtand till the great ſteam is over, and you can look into it. Then pour in all the malt except half a buſhel: let it ſlowly and gradually into the water, and let ſome perſon ſtir it all the while, that there may not be the leaſt lump of it together; then ſtrew over the half buſhel that was ſaved out; and thus leave it two hours, covering it up carefully to keep in the ſteam, and filling up between the maſh-tub and outer veſſel with hot water from time to time as it cools.

When the two hours are expired, rub to pieces in the hands three pounds of hops; and tie them up in a coarſe canvaſs bag; put this into the receiver, and then begin to let in the wort from the maſh-tub in a fine

fine ſmall ſtream, running directly upon the hops; and with a whiſk beat the bag in which the hops are lightly, to promote their firſt moiſtening in the liquor. As this ſtream is running, obſerve the other water. We ordered the fire to be damped when the firſt half was drawn off; and by this time the fire being kept low, this water will be about as hot as the water in the maſh-tub was when the malt was put in. Briſk up the fire by one ſtirring, to make it a little hotter, and then run it off by degrees upon the grains; as the firſt wort is run off into the receiver. Thus, when the quantity of one maſhing is got into the receiver, the ſecond quantity of water will be in the tub. Let this ſtand two hours as the firſt did, keeping up a regular heat, and covering it; only take care to ſtir it very well together, but without beating when it is firſt put together; and in the ſame manner to take off the covering, and ſtir them once more at the

the end of the firſt half hour. All this while the firſt wort will ſtand upon the hops; and, when the two hours are expired, this ſecond wort is to be let off from the maſh-tub to the firſt in the receiver in a large ſtream. The grains will be very well exhauſted by this management; and the worts will be ſtrong, with all the virtue of the malt.

Let the worts ſtand in the receiver one hour, in which time they will let fall a ſmall but coarſe ſediment. Then the whole, except this ſediment, muſt be got into the copper, together with the bag of hops; for tho' there have been two maſhings, there need be but one boiling. As this drink will not have time for ſettling in the caſk like the October or ſtrong beer, all poſſible care is to be taken to clear it in the wort. For this reaſon the wort is not to be pumped out of this receiver into the copper, as was directed in the brewing of October; but care ſhould be taken in in time to raiſe the receiver upon a foot, ſo that the wort can be drawn out of it by a cock placed an inch from the bottom.

The clear wort muſt be put into the copper with the hops, and boiled about eighteen minutes; the exact time muſt be known from the eye and taſte, becauſe it varies conſiderably in different brewings, from the weather, the nature of the malt, and other cauſes.

It muſt be then let into the upper cooler; and, after ſtanding an hour, it muſt be drawn from that into the lower; leaving the ſettlement carefully behind. In this ſecond cooler it muſt ſtand till it is perfectly cold, if the brewing be in ſummer; otherwiſe it need only ſtand till it is milk-warm.

Then it muſt be let off into the working-tun, ſtill leaving the ſettlement behind; and the clear wort will be then in perfect good order for working.

These

Theſe ſeveral ſettlements of the wort will be a vaſt advantage to the ale, making it nearly as clear as old ſtrong beer: and the quantity that is loſt will be very trifling. However, it will be proper to make allowance for it at the firſt proportioning of the water; becauſe the brewing is intended to yield a full hogſhead, and there can be no making up of the deficiences, without greatly hurting the drink. Therefore, in the firſt allowance, there muſt be three gallons of water; for each buſhel of malt, allowed for what will be ſoaked up in the grains; and if a half gallon to the buſhel, that is, four gallons for this quantity, be allowed farther for this article, it will make up the loſs of all the three ſediments.

The wort being thus got into the tun, the manner of working it is to be in all reſpects the ſame with what we have directed for the other kinds. A quart of yeaſt will be ſufficient, if it is good in its kind; and this is to be be firſt put into a little of the drink in a bowl, and then mixed with the whole. The tun is then to be covered up, and kept to the right degree of working, by the methods before directed. After this the drink is to be got into the caſk, by drawing it clear out of the working-tun, and leaving the full ſediment behind: a ſmall quantity is to be ſaved to ſupply what is loſt in the working in the barrel: after this, when the working is thoroughly over, it is to be ſtopp'd down, and will in a little time be fit to tap. It will be a mild, balſamic, and very wholeſome liquor.

CHAP. XXIII.

Of Brewing Small-beer

MOST families have got into ſo regular a way of brewing their ſmall beer after their ale, that it will be not be eaſy to perſuade them

them out of it: but they may be aſſured, that if they have any value for that kind of drink, it is their intereſt to brew it alone: for the trouble is very little more than the other way, and the drink is incomparably better. The method is very little different from the brewing of any other kind. As to the quantity of malt, or ſtrength of the beer, that is at the pleaſure of the perſon; but, however it is intended in point of ſtrength, the brewing ſhould be performed at once; and all that is made ſhould be of one kind, not a ſtronger firſt, and a weaker afterwards. We ſhall give directions at the rate of two buſhels and a half to the hogſhead, which will make a very excellent kind. Mix two buſhels of amber malt, and half a buſhel of brown: let the whole be ground a little more than is done for ſtronger liquors, but then not fine. Let it be laid out on a floor, or in a cool airy room, eighteen hours, and then ſet on half a hogſhead and

two

two pails of water : this is the proper quantity for the firſt copper, as it will yield a clear half hogſhead of wort. Put into the copper a handful of hops, as much ſalt as will lie on a ſhilling, and a race of whole ginger ; ſift over a little malt to keep in the ſpirit, and juſt make it boil : let it out into the maſh-tub, and let it ſtand to be ſomewhat cooler than for the ſtronger kinds of beer ; then pour in the malt, except about a peck ; and ſtir it a good while very carefully together, not beating it about haſtily to break it, but mixing it very well with the liquor : then ſift on the malt that was ſaved out, through a coarſe ſieve, and cover it up ; let it ſtand two hours, then rub to pieces a pound and a half of hops, and tie them up in a coarſe bag : put them into the receiver, and let the wort run out upon them, in a ſmall ſtream. While this maſh is ſtanding, the ſame quantity of water muſt be brought to a due degree of heat.

head. It ſhould be ſomewhat hotter than the firſt; and when the maſh-tub is drained pretty near dry, this muſt be let in. It is to ſtand two hours as the other did, and then to be run off to the reſt in the receiver.

When the grains are well drained, the liquor is to be put into the copper with the hops; and it ſhould boil about half an hour: for more boiling is neceſſary, for theſe ſmall worts, than for the ſtrong; nor does it do them ſuch miſchief. After this the working is to be managed as in other caſes; and the beer will be capable of keeping to a perfect fineneſs; and will far exceed that ordinary and poor kind, which it is poſſible to make after other drinks. When ſuch ſmall beer has ſtood to a due fineneſs, there is no wholeſomer liquor. I remember to have drank at Sir CRISP GASCOIGNE's, ſmall beer, which I think was made in this way, and kept a due time, which every one allowed exceeded in

G plea-

pleaſantneſs, any ſmall drink of malt whatſoever.

CHAP. XXIV.

Of Brewing of Porter.

NOTHING has occaſioned more diſpute or more diverſity of opinions, than the affair of porter. It is a drink in a manner peculiar to London; and which has been attempted in vain in many other parts of the kingdom: it would be a great advantage if this drink could be brewed, in our great trading towns, eſpecially. And the purpoſe of this chapter is to lead the way to that benefit: firſt by ſhewing the miſtakes of thoſe who fancy the brewing is by any natural means limited to London; and, ſecondly, by giving a plain method by which porter has been brewed in a private family. Finally, as this, tho' real porter, is, nor ever will be, entirely equal to the fineſt that is made

at

at public brew-houſes, we ſhall give the reaſon of that; which is principally owing to the great quantity brewed together, and in a great meaſure alſo to the conveniences of thoſe brew-houſes. The reſult, we hope, will be, that private families may if they pleaſe brew porter for their own drinking; and that thoſe who have an inclination to attempt it in the public and larger way, at a diſtance from the metropolis, may ſet about it upon a rational foundation.

CHAP. XXV.

Of the Ingredients of Porter.

AS to any thing particular in the ingredients of porter, it is idle to fancy it. All beer is made of malt, hops and water; and the particular additions uſed to the porter are only two, iſinglaſs, and the juice of elder-berries. This I have a right to ſpeak with ſome aſſurance, having had the opportunity of talking with a gentleman, once concerned in this trade, but who now having left it off with a fair fortune, is above deceiving me, as much as he is above being deceived himſelf. What is thought by the common people to be oxe's blood, is nothing but the elder-juice before-mentioned; and the other ingredient is only beaten iſinglaſs, well diſſolved, and perfectly fine.

As to the water, any ſoft water will do; and in general the ſofter it is, the better. Here is an advantage that private have over public brewers; for the concerns of the latter being ſo large they cannot attend to thoſe ſmall niceties, that a private perſon can; but all they can do is to chuſe a proper water in general, and then to take it, and uſe it as it comes. The malt, we have obſerved already, is a high-dried kind, made of very ordinary barley, dried with culm. There would be no difficulty in any perſon's having this made at a common malſter's; nor indeed is there any neceſſity even for

that

that trouble, ſince it is ſold ready-made, under the name of *Porter-malt*, in many places. As to the hops, all that is neceſſary is chuſing the beſt of their kind. A careful maſhing is then a great article; and for the reſt, it is no way different from the common practice in making all other malt-liquors.

CHAP. XXVI.

To brew Porter in a Private Family.

TAKE eight buſhels of porter-malt, or any other very high-dried brown malt. Let it be ground carefully, ſo as only to crack the grains, not to let out the flour. Lay it in a cool place two days and one night. Then ſet on a hogſhead of ſoft water, and ſo much more as will allow for waſte, according to the directions before given. This muſt be covered with a head of malt, to keep in the

G 3 ſpirit;

ſpirit; and, when it has once boiled up, the fire muſt be immediately damped, and about one third part of it muſt be let into the maſh-tub. Then it is to ſtand till cool. It muſt be cooler than what is required in the common method of brewing; and then the malt to be poured gradually in. While it is pouring in, it muſt be ſtirred very well about; and, when all is in, a perſon ſhould work it ſtill round and round, firſt one way and then another, for half an hour together; but this muſt be done gently, not to bruiſe or break the malt. The water in the copper ſhould be kept at a little more than the heat of that which is uſed for the maſh in common brewing: and when the malt has been thus maſhed a full half hour, there muſt be as much more let in as will make it in the whole ſomething more than half the quantity of the water This muſt all be very well ſtirred once together, and then covered with the malt that was left out for that purpoſe: it is then to be be covered close up in the vessel to keep in the heat, and thus to stand two hours and a half.

Then bruise four pound of hops between the hands, and tie them up in a bag; put them into the receiver or under-back, and let the wort run out upon them in a fine, small stream. When this is running, stir up the fire under the copper, and make the remaining water considerably hot; then run it on upon the grains, when the other is nearly run off; and, after stirring them well about, cover the mash-tub, and let them stand two hours more. Then run this second wort upon the first, with the hops still in it; and let them stand till quite cold.

Then lay a cask a little above the bottom of the receiver, draw off the whole directly, so as to leave the coarser that has settled behind; pour the wort into the copper, put in the hops with it; and boil them about twenty minutes. Then let off the wort into the upper back or cooler; in which let it ſtand till ſo cool that you can bear to put your hand in it: then draw it off (leaving again the ſediment behind) into the other, or under cooler.

In this let it ſtand till only milk-warm, and then prepare for working; put into a bowl three pints of good and moderately thick yeaſt; work this gently about with a little of the wort, and then put it into the tun. Let the wort out of the cooler run gradually into the tun, ſo as to blend with this, and to leave its own ſediment behind.

Thus there will be the pure wort cleared by theſe ſeveral ſettlements, and well mixed with the yeaſt in the tun; then let it be cloſe covered up, and gradually there will be ſeen to gather upon it a fine mantling head, which will thicken every hour, and at laſt riſe in waves, and then in little curls. This is the perfection of its fermentation. The tun muſt be uncovered from time to to time to look down into this; and when it has arrived at this head, which will usually be in about six and thirty hours, it will be time to have the cask quite ready. This fine head will soon begin to fall; and then it must be drawn off into the cask, leaving again what settlement it has made in the tun.

A small quantity must be saved to fill up as it wastes in the working, and the full time allowed for this last fermentation in the barrel: then a little isinglass, dissolved as before directed, must be put into the cask, and a quart and half a pint of elder-berry. When these last ingredients are put in, the vessel is to be left with a little opening at the vent-hole two days, and then stopped up entirely. The rule for tapping is when it is fine: and that generally happens in about fifteen days. If it be then drank from the cask, it will be very bright, clear, and pleasant, well-coloured, and of a good body. It will have all the flavour of porter; tho' not the ſound and peculiar taſte of what has been kept a conſiderable time in a large body; which is the caſe with moſt of the porter that is drank at the famous houſes in London.

The flavour which a mixture of elder-juice gives even in this ſmall quantity, is truly that which we expect in fine old porter; and, what is very ſingular, it is of the ſame kind with that which porter gets by being long kept in a large quantity. This muſt not appear wonderful; for in chemiſtry, and even in the common affairs of life, we find the taſte of peculiar things may be given to a mixture by thoſe which ſeems of a very different nature: in particular, the root of maſterwort, with common fennel ſeed, gives its tincture the flavour of ſaſſafras. Other inſtances might be given, which indeed are frequent, tho' they are not known. This may be ſufficient.

The

The other great article of time, and keeping in a body, is what a private family cannot have opportunity of doing; and 'tis for that reaſon, and that only, the public brewed porter will always be ſuperior. The brewers of this liquor have large caſks, in which it is kept two years and more: and in thoſe it undergoes a laſt fermentation; which, as it is ſlight and ſlow, produces no other change than mellowing of the drink; that, is a perfect mixture of the malt and hops: it laſts a long time, and conſequently the effect is greater: in fine, this laſt fermentation, perfect reſt, and a cool air from good cellarage, produce a fineneſs and clean ſound taſte in this liquor; which is what we admire, and what is not to be found in any other; becauſe the ſame degree of keeping in any other kind than a brown malt beer would ſoften it, but take off the ſpirit.

Another advantage the great brewers have, which private familie can-

G 6 not

not, this is an opportunity of correcting the faults of one butt of their porter, by means of another. It is in this their great practice aſſiſts them ; and it does the ſame in their brewing : for their judgment directs to mix and bring this to a proper taſte and ſtrength ; otherwiſe, to an unexperienced perſon, they would ſeem to do it wildly. Thus, in brewing porter, they make three and ſometimes four maſhes ; ſtrengthening them with a little freſh malt, or running them as they call it a greater length, that is, making more beer from the ſame malt, according to their pleaſure. Theſe ſeveral worts they mix, and make the whole of ſuch a ſtrength as experience ſhews them porter ought to have ; and this they work and barrel up accordingly.

In the ſame manner, if a butt of porter be too mild, they will throw into it a ſmall quantity of ſome that is very ſtrong and too ſtale ; firſt diſſolving in it a little iſinglaſs. This pro-

produces a new tho' ſlight fermentation; and the liquor, in eighteen or twenty days, fines down, and has the expected flavour. Theſe, and many ſuch advantages, none but the public brewers can have: and therefore none but they can brew this beer in that degree of perfection. We do not propoſe the brewing it in private families in London. But the extent of this enquiry into its nature is, that thoſe who prefer this to other malt-liquors, and live in places where it cannot conveniently be bought, may brew it for themſelves; and that ſuch as may intend to erect public breweries for it, may proceed with regularity. The conſtruction of thoſe large brew-houſes, where it is uſually made, favours alſo greatly the excellence of the drink: and this is the third article of which it was propoſed to treat in this enquiry.

CHAP.

CHAP. XXVII.

Of the Conſtruction of a great Brew-houſe.

IN erecting a large work of this kind, every thing is to be conſidered, that can ſave the labour of the people employed; for as every thing is done in quantities, the difficulty of removing the ingredients from place to place would be very great, but for the help of ſuch early care. There is alſo an advantage in the conſtructing of a brew-houſe merely as a brew-houſe; becauſe it may be better calculated to anſwer the purpoſe, than when any part of a houſe is employed, or ever ſo well fitted up for that purpoſe. A brew-houſe ſhould always ſtand ſeparate from all other buildings; and the place of the veſſels ſhould be ſo contrived, that the liquor may be conveyed from one of them to the other; and ſo on in the

the whole courſe: not only without the labour of carriage, as was done in the old way of private brewing; but even without pumping. Herein conſiſts in ſome degree the difference between a well-contrived public, and private brew-houſe; that many things may be done by hand in the one, which cannot by any means be ſo in the other. Thus the pumping from the copper to the cooler, as they do from the receiver to the copper, is no great matter in a ſmall quantity, and when the brewing is but once or twice in a year; but it becomes an article of importance, when the quantity is very great, and the brewing continual.

Free air is another great article in a brew-houſe; and for this purpoſe the upper part of it ſhould always be built with lattice work, not with a ſolid wall, except on one ſide.

This gives a particular direction alſo for the ſituation and aſpect of a brew-houſe; ſince, tho' the air is to be let

let in, the ſun ſhould by all means be kept out.

Therefore the brew-houſe ſhould be ſo placed, that the entire wall may ſtand to the ſouth-weſt, to keep off the ſun of the middle of the day, and of the afternoon; and the place for the copper ſhould be againſt this wall, at a height of about eleven foot above the ground.

There muſt be conveniences for the grinding of the malt; for here every thing ſhould be done at home; and the mill-ſtones muſt be placed high, ſo that the malt, when ground, may be conveyed eaſily into the places where it will be wanted.

The brew-houſe is to be divided into two floors, as it were; the one, the lower of them, being wrought up with an entire wall, and the upper on the three ſides with lattice, or open work; only the back being entire.

The labour of grinding is to be done by a horſe; and the ſame creature, by good contrivance, may raiſe the

the water by the pumps, and convey the wort out of the receiver into the copper, by ſuch another machine: thus vaſt labour may be ſaved.

CHAP. XXVIII.

Of the Diſpoſition of the Veſſels.

THE old brewers uſed to place their copper a little above the level of the ground; and conſequently the reſt of the veſſels were ſo diſpoſed, as to be ſubjected to great inconvenience, and to bring on the neceſſity of a deal of labour. The receiver from the maſh-tub was forced to be placed below the level of the ground; and in conſequence was a receptacle for all ſorts of dirt, and the labour of pumping was the greater. In the placing of the veſſels a great deal of labour is eaſily ſaved, and all theſe depend upon the copper. Therefore its ſituation ſhould never be at a leſs height than what I have nam-

ed,

ed, nor need it ever be higher. There will thus be a deſcent ſufficient for all the purpoſes that can be anſwered that way; for, in ſpite of all poſſible contrivance, there will ſtill remain in a brew-houſe ſomething to be done by pumping. This comes from the nature of the work: for as a deſcent, for inſtance, is required to carry the liquor from the copper to the maſh-tub; and the ſame liquor when made into wort is to be conveyed from the receiver, which is ſtill lower than the maſh-tub, into the copper again; it cannot be but that this muſt be by a conſiderable aſcent; and therefore can be only done by pumping: but as the horſe which grinds the malt may be made to perform this ſervice, it is of little conſequence.

When there are two coppers in a brew-houſe, they ſhould be placed both againſt the back or entire walls of the brew-houſe, with their fire-places ſo near one another, that one perſon can manage both the fires. There muſt be be a long arm from the bottom or near the bottom of the copper, with a cock of a large bore at the end, for discharging the water into the mash-tub; and the same contrivance will answer also for running out the wort, when it has been boiled with the hops, into the coolers.

The mash-tub must be very large, and it must be placed as little as possible below the level of the bottom of the copper; because, what is discharged from the copper into that, is to go again from the receiver into the copper; and the less the ascent thither is, the easier will be the labour, and the better the conveyance.

The cooler must also be large, and they must be all placed upon one level; for if otherwise, the steam from the lower would heat those above; and in part defeat the very purpose for which they were used. This is another difference between the public and the private Brew-house: each in its way being accommodated to.

to its purpoſes. The working-tun is to be proportioned to the reſt; indeed, properly ſpeaking, the ſize of all the veſſels, as well as their place, is to be deduced from the copper, for that is the firſt utenſil and object of proportion.

The method of work in ſuch a brew-houſe is to be this: the ſoft water being laid in from the water-works, the cocks are to open over the coppers: and, for the pump-water that is wanted, either in deficience of theſe conveniencies, or from the nature of the drink to be brewed, is to be raiſed by the mill-horſe that grinds the corn. The apparatus of which every ſmith now knows. The grinding of the malt is the next article; and this is made to fall directly into the maſh-tub; for there is a great ſquare trough brought down from the place where the mill-ſtones deliver the malt, which reaches into the maſh-tub; and conſequently the corn, as it is ground, runs at at once into the tub where it is to be mafhed.

This is now a favourite contrivance among the brewers; but, to fpeak freely, it is wrong: in the old way, the malt, when ground, ufed to be received into a great bin, whence it was afterwards handed by bafkets into the mafh-tub. This labour is faved; but in brewing, as in other arts, when the fcheme of improvements is on foot, it is ufually carried too far. Thus, in the old way, when the wort was boiled with the hops, they ufed to pump it up into one large back, placed at a confiderable height; and, from this, it ran into all the others to cool. The new improvements have contrived it fo, that the wort, when boiled, is conveyed at once into the coolers from the copper by means of the long arm; and this without the labour of pumping, as well as without the firft or high back. No body will difpute the value of this improvement; but they went too far, who, upon this plan, contrived the

the grinding to be delivered at once to the mash-tub, and saved the bin, which used to be placed to receive the ground malt, and the labour of handing it in baskets from thence into the mash-tub: for this improvement, as it is called, brings us to a necessity of brewing with malt directly from the mill, which is always hot and rank in some degree; and deprives us of the advantage it would get in lying four and twenty hours or more to soften and mellow after grinding: the benefit of which is known to every one.

In large brew-houses, I am sensible, every thing is obliged to be done quick; but this time of mellowing the malt after grinding, ought to be allowed without any inconvenience; and, as to the labour of handing it from the bin into the mash-tub by baskets, that, I think, may be very easily avoided. I would propose, that there be a bin as was usual in the old brew-houses, and that the malt be discharged into this immediately as it is ground, there being

being a trough or great ſpout running from the place where the ſtones are into the bin for that purpoſe. In this bin I would have the malt remain four and twenty hours after grinding; and, as the mill-ſtones are now very rightly placed high, the bin may alſo be ſo much above the maſh-tub, that the malt, after lying its time to mellow, may run into the maſh-tub through ſuch another trough or ſpout, without any labour of the hand. This would ſave all poſſible waſte as much as the other, and the malt would go into the maſh-tub, not only mellowed, but with all perfection.

The arm of the copper lets the water into the maſh-tub; and experience and long practice ſhews the common brewers what is the due degree of heat it ſhould have, without looking to ſee their faces in it.

When the wort is run into the receiver, and is to be got back into the copper for boiling with the hops, this is done by a pump which is worked

by

by the mill-horſe: and it is the only aſcent the liquor has in the whole courſe of the brewing, and conſequently is the only part of the work that requires this labour. When the wort is boiled, it is diſcharged into the backs or coolers by means of the arm fixed to the copper, without the leaſt trouble: and the conveyance of it from theſe into the great working-tun, is plain and eaſy; for there is to each of theſe a leaden pipe of two inch bore, which goes to the working-tun, and, by a cock there, can let in the wort at pleaſure: this ſhortens that labour extremely.

Theſe leaden pipes are not placed quite ſo low as to let out the ſediment; but there is another opening in the cooler, which is ſtopped with a wooden plug, and which being opened, lets out all the bottom of the cooler, is ſwept clean, and the whole is let thro' this hole: though foul, it is not loſt; for it is to be let into a piece of flannel tied to a hoop, and, draining thro'

this,

this, the whole clear liquor is catched in a tub, and afterwards put to the rest, being no way different when thus strained. Thus no part of the wort is lost; and yet this method saves the mixing of the gross sediments with the beer; which always gives it a heavy taste in the beginning, and a tendency to sourness afterwards. It is of great importance not to admit these sediments of gross and earthy matter, for they bring on changes in the drink, even after it is in the cask, upon every great change of weather: and yet it would be too great a loss to waste the whole.

All that can be got from the several mashings being thus conveyed to the working-tun, no more than the common care is needful farther, to see that it has the due time and proper degree of fermentation, and then to run it into the casks, where time and good cellarage will do all the rest, producing that excellent as well as pleasant

H liquor,

liquor, which we ſee at the beſt houſes.

CHAP. XXIX.

Of Dorcheſter Beer.

A Peculiar fine kind of ſtrong beer brewed in and about Dorcheſter has long been famous; and has indeed deſerved to be ſo. From being celebrated upon the ſpot, it has been ſent into all parts of the kingdom; and is now one of the firſt beers in repute in England. There are ſome advantages on the place which tend to the excellence of this drink; and, from great practice, the brewers there, and thereabouts, have a perfect knowledge of the making it: but this kind of drink is not limited abſolutely to the place. We ſhall teach the brewer how he may make it any where; and that in ſo exact a manner, that the palate of the Dorcheſter brewer himſelf ſhould

ſhould not find out the difference. If the reader ſhould chuſe to carry the particulars of this kind of brewing alſo to other drinks, he would in general find them uſeful : but this would be confounding the ſeveral kinds with one another. It is better to keep up the diſtinction, and to let porter be porter, October be October, and Dorcheſter be Dorcheſter, than to give one a flavour for another, and have no real difference among them.

Dorcheſter beer is a kind of ſtrong malt-liquor diſtinguiſhed from all others by its briſkneſs, ſoftneſs, and pure taſte. The ingredients of which it is made are the ſame with thoſe of all other kinds of malt liquor; and therefore the peculiarity muſt be owing to the management. One thing alone is particular in nature upon the ſpot, that is the water : but, as it will be eaſy to ſee what is the occaſion of that, it will be eaſy alſo to imitate it.

H 2 It

It has been thought the Thames water was peculiar to porter; but we have ſhewn that to be an error: on the other hand, it is true, that a water impregnated with chalk is eſſential to the Dorcheſter beer. The country thereabouts abounds with chalk, and the ſprings which ſupply their breweries all riſe in chalk. It is to this the ſoftneſs of the Dorcheſter beer is owing; the ſpirit or natural flavour is owing to their way of managing it. There is this original ſpirit in all water; but the common methods of brewing diſſipate and waſte it; whereas that uſed in making this particular drink, preſerves and detains it.

'Tis neceſſary, however, that we firſt underſtand the nature of the water itſelf; for though it is a chalky kind, we ſhould be deceived, if we ſuppoſed all waters that came off a chalk would anſwer the ſame purpoſe. We have in England many kinds of chalk, differing in degree of of hardneſs; ſome approaching to the firmneſs of ſtone, others being ſoft as marle. The farmers who uſe chalk as a manure, know this difference very well; for they find the ſoft chalk anſwer in the way of marle; whereas the hard does but very poorly ſerve their uſes. It is the ſame in this caſe. Water that riſes among a ſoft marly chalk is always ſoftened by it; and ſhews this quality by lathering finely with ſoap, and boiling garden-ſtuff freely and excellently: on the other hand, water which riſes among the hard ſtony chalks, will be often as harſh and hard itſelf as that which iſſues from an abſolute rock. It will curdle inſtead of lathering with ſoap, and will harden garden-ſtuff. Some have ſuppoſed that the chalk gave it that harſh quality: but this is not the fact; the water paſſes through and among the maſſes of this chalk, and is not altered by it at all, but riſes like the waters of other ſprings.

This obſervation has appeared needful, becauſe a chalky water is eſſential to fine Dorcheſter beer; and, unleſs its nature were underſtood, there might be a great error in the choice, even after the fact was known.

Therefore, if the brewer lives where there is a ſoft chalky water, he need not fear ſucceſs. But, as this is not the caſe often, we ſhall mention how the deficiency may be ſupplied. Let a load of ſoft chalk, a little broke to pieces, be ſtrewed over the bottom of one of the large backs or coolers, and upon this pump as much ſpring-water as will more than half fill it; then let in about half as much ſoft water as there was pump-water, and let the chalk be ſtirred a little with an oar. Then leave it four and twenty hours, and the water will be ready for brewing. It will be much clearer than it was when put in; for all the foulneſs of the ſoft water will be carried down

down to the chalk; and it will be juſt as ſoft as that commonly uſed at Dorcheſter and there about is. This water being drawn off, will be ready for the brewing; and the ſame chalk, being taken out of the cooler and ſpread to drain, will ſerve afterwards for the ſame purpoſe, even better than at firſt. Chalk ſeems ſo far of the nature of quickſilver, that it will communicate a certain quality to water without any change in itſelf, and will therefore continue to impregnate new waters over and over again in the ſame manner.

CHAP. XXX.

The Method of Brewing.

THOUGH the Docheſter water is favourable to the brewing that excellent kind of drink, a great deal alſo depends upon the method of the work, which is different from that of other brewing, and muſt be carefully followed, even in in the leaſt articles, by thoſe who expect ſucceſs.

As to the quality of the malt, that muſt be determined by the intended ſtrength of the beer, and it is in every one's pleaſure to vary his accordingly: but as directions are no way ſo well underſtood as by bringing them to ſome particular ſtint of quantity, we ſhall fix upon the brewing it at fourteen buſhels to the hogſhead, and give the rule for making this quantity at a brewing; the which every one may extend and enlarge at pleaſure.

Chuſe, for this purpoſe, eight buſhels of excellent pale malt, and ſix of amber malt, ſweet dried with fine clear fuel; grind this together, and let it ſtand in the ſacks eighteen hours after the grinding: then ſet on a copper of the water before directed, containing ſo much, that, beſide what the malt ſoaks up, there will be a good half-hogſhead for the wort.

wort. Sift over this a good head of malt, and let it heat till it is of that degree of heat which is in water which has been boiled and stood till one can see one's face in it. The great care is to have the water so hot as to open the pores of the malt, and yet not hot enough to scald it. The temper just mentioned, when a man can see his face in it after boiling and standing is very exactly what we mean; though this method of overheating and then cooling, is a bad way of getting at it: because the finest and freshest part of the water is lost in that great evaporation. We know all boiling hardens water, and what we want in this is to be soft; why then should we use a method that is quite contrary to our intention? What must be done is this: he who undertakes to brew this beer, must be well acquainted with what degree of heat that is, which water has when he can see his face in it after boiling; and he must heat this

H 5 copper

copper of water to that degree of heat, and no more. There is nothing impoſſible in this; for the common brewers all do it, though in a various manner. They boil their water, and then let in cold till it comes to the degree of heat juſt mentioned: but this way they looſe a part of the ſpirit of the firſt water; and it would evidently be better if they did it in the manner here directed.

When the water in the copper is of this due degree of heat, let it into the maſh-tub, and immediately begin pouring in the malt. Do this ſlowly and carefully, and all the while let it be ſtirred but very gently; a careful hand muſt ſo manage it in the ſtirring, that the malt does not get together in lumps; but this is all, and provided this is done, the leſs ſtiring there is beſide the better. About half a buſhel of the malt muſt be reſerved; and, when the ſtirring of the maſh is finiſhed, this muſt be put over it. Thus the malt will be

in

in a due heat to give out its virtue, and ſecured from evaporation. Thus let it ſtand two hours and a quarter; and, by the end of that time, let another copper of water, containing ſomewhat more than a half-hogſhead, be got to the ſame degree of heat that the firſt was. Then run off the wort out of the maſh-tub into the receiver, upon ſix pounds of very good hops, which have been rubbed in the hands, and are tied up in a coarſe bag.

When this wort is drained off, gently ſtir in the cap of freſh malt that was put over the maſh with the reſt, and then let in ſome of the water from the copper in a moderate ſtream. Stir the grains gently with this, and let them ſtand a little while; then run this off into the receiver, as the former whole quantity was, by a ſmall ſtream; then let in ſo much more water out of the copper: it will be a little hotter by this time, and ſo it ſhould, but ſtill not too

H 6 hot;

hot; gently ſtir the grains with this, and after a little time let it run off: then let in the reſt of the water of the copper, and ſtir all gently together again; cover this up, let it ſtand a quarter of an hour, and then run it off to the reſt.

Thus the malt will be entirely drained of its whole virtue; and there will be in the receiver a quantity of wort ſufficient to allow for all waſte, and yet to make a hogſhead of the beer. The hops will have been a very conſiderable time ſoaking in this, and therefore will quickly give out their virtue by boiling. The whole wort, with the hops, muſt now be got into the copper, and very leiſurely heated till it comes to boiling; then it muſt be boiled briſkly a quarter of an hour; and after this the hops are to be taken out. Then the wort is to be boiled alone five or ſix minutes; and after this it muſt be drawn off into the coolers, and lie ſhallow at their bottom.

bottom. Let ſome perſon, from time to time, ſtir the wort gently in the coolers, and let it remain in them till it is perfectly cold: for the method of this brewing will bring on a fermentation without the aſſiſtance of any heat in the wort, and this will be ſufficient for all the purpoſes of purifying and keeping; and as there is no heat in the liquor, none of its ſpirit will be loſt.

When the wort is thoroughly cold, ſtir it up entirely together, ſo as not to leave any ſediment; but run it off entire as it is into the working-tun. The motion and the mixture of the ſediment with the clear liquor will create a kind of fermentation in the beer before the yeaſt comes to it. Nature muſt be allowed her courſe in this; there will riſe to the top of the wort a white head: when this is fully formed, it muſt be ſkimed clean off and thrown away, and the liquor will then be in a right condition to receive the yeaſt.

About

About three pints of moderately thick yeaſt will be neceſſary to give this beer a thorough working. This muſt be freſh and fine: it muſt be mixed firſt with a little of the wort, and then put to the whole. Cover up the working-tun, and let it ſtand till the head is perfect upon the wort. Then beat it in, and cover up the tun again. This is all that will be needed in the working: when the head falls, let it be cleared off for the caſk. To this purpoſe the head and the ſettlement muſt both be ſeparated from the pure wort; the head muſt be ſkimed off, and the ſettlement left behind, by drawing it out of the tun by a cock ſix inches above the bottom.

When it is got clear into the veſſel, let ſome be alſo ſaved to fill it up, as a ſmall quantity will be waſted by this laſt fermentation. This is to be let in from time to time, ſo as to keep the veſſel quite full; and it muſt be by means of a funnel with

with a long ſpout, that it may be let gradually to the liquor, without diſturbing the head. When the fermentation in the caſk is over, it muſt be ſtopped cloſe down, and ſtand to mellow all winter, for autumn is the beſt time for this kind of brewing. Although the ſettling has been large in the working-tun, from the letting in the wort with all its dregs out of the coolers; yet there will remain in it ſo much of the finer part of that which would have been left in the cooler, if it had been drawn off clear, as will ſerve excellently for it to feed upon, as the brewer expreſſes it; and this will ſupply the place of all thoſe mixtures which are directed to be put into beers for that purpoſe. It is with this intent that the bottoms are ſtirred up and mixed with the wort, when it is diſcharged from the cooler into the working-tun, in this particular method of brewing; and it is owing to this that the Dorcheſter beer has a peculiar

peculiar taſte of the grounds, like what is called the biting of the yeaſt; which is extremely agreeable, becauſe it is very moderate.

As the weather grows warm in the following ſpring, there will be in this, as in all other beers, a new, though ſlight, fermentation. The vent-hole muſt be opened to give way to this; and it muſt continue open till it is thoroughly over; then it is to be ſtopped, and to ſtand till the cool weather comes again. Then, by pegging the caſk, draw out a little, and if it is not fine, ſtay longer, and draw a little more to try it: when it is tolerably clear, put in a little iſinglaſs, to compleat the fining of it, and it will be fit for bottling in a very ſhort time after, or for drinking from the caſk, if that be rather choſen. The quantity of iſinglaſs need be only an ounce and half; it ſhould be deſolved in a gallon of the beer, drawn for that purpoſe; and, when put to the reſt, it muſt be left

open

open while the new fermentation laſts, and then ſtopped cloſe.

CHAP. XXXI.

Of Oat Ale.

WE meet with very poor liquor often under the name of oat ale; and, indeed, very little is really brewed from the grain from whence it has its name. Bottled ſmall beer is what we commonly get when we call for this liquor; and even that is ſeldom brewed on purpoſe: but real oat ale is a very different liquor. It differs from all others in two moſt eſſential articles, for it is made from a different grain, and is brewed cold. When thus made it is briſker than any thing that is ſold under its name, and has a great many other good qualities. No malt-liquor is ſo agreeable at meals, and nothing is more wholeſome. We ſhall give the reader an exact

exact knowledge of what it is, that he may know how far from the deſcription every thing is that he meets with at public houſes under that name: and ſhall then give the true method of brewing it; which is ſo eaſy that I ſhould think none who had a brew-houſe would omit to make this particular liquor.

Oat ale, when genuine and well brewed, is a fine, ſpirited and balſamic liquor; it is very pale in colour, briſk, and yet extremely ſoft to the taſte; it ſparkles in the glaſs, and riſes to a fine creamy head; it is perfectly clear, and free from all ill flavour. By this deſcription we ſhall eaſily ſee, that what is commonly ſold is not genuine. The true way to make it is this.

The malt muſt be made of the fineſt white oats, without any mixture; and the water muſt be clean, and yet not hard; that of a fine running brook is beſt: but, if ſuch cannot be had, the ſofteſt water that can

can be got, muſt be uſed, and it muſt have time to ſettle. With ſuch malt and ſuch water, the fineſt oat ale may be brewed; but the quantity ſhould be no more than can be uſed in about two months, for when it is the fineſt that can be it will keep no longer.

Take eight buſhels of this oat malt, perfectly clean and ſweet; let it be ground very lightly, juſt to crack the corns, and no more; then lay it in a heap, in a cool, but dry, airy room, for two days and nights; then put it into a large maſh-tub, and pour upon it fifty gallons of cold water, ſuch as has been juſt directed. Stir it about, juſt enough to prevent the malt from ſticking together in lumps, and then cover it up. Open the maſh-tub after one hour, and ſtir it all together again; then cover it up as before; repeat this afterwards once in two hours, till the whole has been maſhing, without any heat, thirteen hours. Then tie a piece of flannel

flannel looſely over the cock of the maſh-tub, and prepare the hops. Chuſe the fineſt and freſheſt hops; two pounds and a quarter are the proper quantity for this brewing. Rub them to pieces in the hands, and tie them up in a piece of coarſe canvaſs; lay them in the receiver, under the maſh-tub, and let the wort out of the tub run upon them in a ſmall ſtream through the flannel. Give it time to drain thoroughly; and, after it is all in, let it ſtand four hours; then pour the wort through a flannel, faſtened to a hoop, into the working-tun; and put to it a pint and half of fine thickiſh yeaſt. Mix this firſt with a little of the wort, and then with the whole; cover the working-tub very carefully, and a fermentation will preſently come on: let the head riſe fairly, and let it work briſkly for two days. Then ſkim off the head, and draw it off out of the tun into the caſk, by a cock placed five inches above

the

the bottom of the tun; and let it this time alſo run through flannel. Thus will the drink be got quite clear and fine into the caſk; there it will have a new, but very ſlight fermentation; and this alſo muſt be allowed its regular time, the veſſel being kept filled up with ſome of the wort ſaved for that purpoſe. When this ſlight working is thoroughly over, the veſſel is to be ſtopped down faſt, and the drink muſt be allowed a fortnight to mellow and ſettle perfectly. In that time the hop and wort will thoroughly blended together, ſo as to make but one united taſte, and the drink will be as clear as the pureſt water, and very lightly coloured.

Let the bottles be perfectly clean, and thoroughly dry; draw off the drink ſlowly and gradually into them; and while one fills, let another cork. All this muſt be done with as little motion as is poſſible; and the corks ſhould not now be thruſt

thruſt down perfectly faſt. The bottles ſhould be held as little as can be in the hand, and moved gently without ſhaking: as they are corked they ſhould be ſet regularly upon the floor; and it will be beſt if this be in a place where water can be thrown over them, and run off freely.

As ſoon as the whole is bottled off, pump ſeveral pails of water, and throw it, as cold as can be, upon the bottles. This will check any tendency to heat or fermentation, which the motion in bottling might have brought on.

The next day drive in the corks faſt, and then once more throw water over the bottles; and, as ſoon as it is run off, ſet them where they are to remain for uſe.

CHAP.

CHAP. XXXII.

The Brewing of Pale Home-Brewed.

BY the term home-brewed we underſtand no other than a mild ale, which has not come out of the hands of the common brewer. Such as is generally underſtood by this term, is what we have deſcribed already, under the general name of *Ale*; but, in ſome parts of the kingdom, they brew a very pleaſant and wholeſome ale, of moderate ſtrength, from pale malt alone; and as there is ſomething particular in the management, we ſhall give it at large.

Grind eight buſhels of pale malt, which makes the hogſhead of this drink; let it be broke a little finer than the brown malts are broke in grinding, and lay it to mellow four and twenty hours; then ſet on ſpring-water for the firſt maſhing, which ſhould be about two-thirds of of a hogſhead. Sift ſome malt over the ſurface, and heat it till it is very near boiling; let it out into the maſh-tub, and, after it has ſtood five minutes, pour in the ſeven buſhels of malt, ſtirring it very well together, to prevent its getting into lumps. It is intended that the water ſhould be mixed with the malt much warmer than in other brewings. When it is very well mixed, take half the buſhel that was left out, and ſtrew it evenly over the maſh. Let this ſtand two hours and a half, and in the mean time have more hot water ready; and at the end of this time let in about fifteen gallons, without letting out any of the wort already in the maſh-tub. Stir the whole very well together again, and put upon it the other half buſhel of malt; cover this up, and let it ſtand as before only one hour.

Then put one pound and a half of hops into a canvaſs bag, rub them well between the hands, put them into

into the receiver; and let the wort drain upon them with a ſmall ſtream. Have more water ready hot in the copper; and when this wort is run off, let in as much to the grains as will ſerve to make up a hogſhead, with what is already run off, allowing ſufficient for waſte.

Let this ſtand an hour and a half, and in the mean time boil off the firſt wort. Let it boil half an hour with the hops, and about a half quarter of an hour more after they are taken out; then run it off into the coolers. In this time the laſt maſh will be near finiſhed. Prepare for this a pound and half more hops, as for the firſt, putting them into a looſe and coarſe canvaſs bag, and rubbing them to pieces between the hands: put them into the receiver, and let this wort alſo run off from the maſh-tub, in a ſmall ſtream. When all is run off, let the hops remain in it a quarter of an hour, in the receiver, and then put them and

I the

the wort together into the copper; boil theſe half an hour, and then run this wort off alſo into the cooler to the other.

The whole is to ſtand there till it is thoroughly cold; and then draw it off clear into the working-tun. Leave all the ſettlement behind in the cooler. Mix about three pints of good yeaſt with a ſmall quantity of the wort, and then put it to the reſt. Cover up the working-tun; and when the head has been at its full heighth, and begins to fall, which will naturally be in two days and a half, draw it off clear into the caſk, keeping out a little to ſupply the waſte of working over in that veſſel.

When the fermentation is thoroughly done, faſten it down, and it will fine of itſelf in about fifteen days; after which it may be tapped for preſent drinking, and will prove a very clean, bright, pleaſant and wholeſome beer.

CHAP.

CHAP. XXXIII.

Of the Time of Brewing.

HAVING gone through the article of brewing, there remains only to give ſome general rules as to the ſeaſons of the year fitteſt for this operation, and the beſt manner of keeping malt-liquors in perfection, when we have made them ſo. The firſt article is what comes under the preſent head; and the latter, as it relates to cellarage and the preſerving of beer in the caſk, or in bottles, will afford the ſubjects of the two concluding chapters.

The beſt ſeaſon for brewing ſtrong beer for keeping, is late in the autumn; and 'tis from this circumſtance, theſe malt-liquors have got the general name of October beer. There are two evident reaſons why this time of the year is preferable to all others for the purpoſe; the firſt

I 2 is,

is, becauſe the waters are never in ſo good a condition for brewing; and the other, becauſe the time of keeping theſe liquors being generally at leaſt one year; there is a whole winter for them to fine themſelves after the brewing, and a whole ſummer for that ſecond and moſt natural fermentation, which comes on of itſelf in the liquor, by the heat of the ſpring; and is the only operation whereby the fine part of the malt and hops mellow perfectly together. The month of September is generally rainy; and the rivers, and other bodies of water, are filled after the waſte of ſummer. We have ſaid, in the beginning of this treatiſe, that no water is ſo ſoft as rain; and therefore the rivers, and other reſervoirs, filled at this ſeaſon, are ſofter than at any other time of the year. By the middle or latter end of October, they have been well ſupplied, and the firſt foulneſs is over: it is then therefore their water is in in the greateſt degree of perfection for the brewery.

Beſide this advantage of the goodneſs of water, and the opportunity of the time for keeping, the very temper of the air is ſuited in October to this buſineſs: there is juſt warmth enough remaining in it to bring on a good fermentation, and the following cold ſeaſon prevents the beer from freting in the caſk, at a time when it ſhould be only mellowing and fining.

For theſe reaſons, October is the beſt month for brewing in general; and of all kinds of drink it is the moſt ſuited to the ſtrong beers.

The depth of winter has many diſadvantages in regard to brewing; for the water will not ſo well extract the virtues of the malt, nor will the drink ferment ſo freely and naturally, as when there is a moderate warmth in the air, to aſſiſt the efforts of nature for that purpoſe. When neceſſity obliges us to brew in this cold ſea-

I 3 ſon,

ſon, we find it neceſſary to heat the water to a greater degree than at other times, and yet it performs the buſi-neſs but very imperfectly. The brown malts ſhould be uſed when a brewing is undertaken in this bad time of the year, becauſe they give out their vir-tue more freely than the pale; and becauſe the coldneſs of the air ſooner takes off that great heat theſe kinds get in the drying.

The malt muſt be twelve hours longer between the grinding and the maſhing at this, than at any other ſeaſon of the year; and the maſhing muſt be continued half an hour longer, and the maſh-tub muſt care-fully be kept covered.

In ſummer all the contraries occur in brewing, to what we have here named, for the diſadvantages of the winter-ſeaſon; but then they occur in ſuch extremes, that they are as hurtful on the one hand, as thoſe were on the other. Water in general is hard and dead in ſummer, becauſe there

there have been few ſupplies of rain, and the evaporation of the ſun and air has been very great. We have ſhewn that rain-water ſoftens rivers and ponds; and it has been ſtrongly repreſented, that, in evaporation, the beſt part of the water is always loſt: therefore, what we have ſaid of the deadneſs and hardneſs of ſummer-water is plain to reaſon, as well as to the ſenſes. This is one evident cauſe why thoſe who are curious in their drink, ſhould never brew in the heat of ſummer; and there is another as forcible, which is, that the heat of the weather brings on the fermentation too violently and haſtily, and keeps it up a great deal beyond the proper degree.

Therefore thoſe, who cannot avoid brewing at this ſeaſon, ſhould make no more than is for preſent ſervice; for ſummer-beer will never anſwer for keeping. Another rule is, that they muſt get the ſofteſt and freſheſt water that they can; and, in general,

I 4 river-

river-water is preferable to pond: a leſs degree of heat in the water for maſhing, will anſwer the purpoſe of extracting the virtue of the malt; and leſs yeaſt will bring on a fermentation. The wort ſhould be worked in a broad ſhallow veſſel, not in a deep tun; and it is beſt to divide it into two or more parcels; for the ſmaller body there is of it, the milder will be the fermentation.

The ſpring is a very good ſeaſon for this buſineſs, and comes next to the autumn. Fermentation comes on freely at this ſeaſon, but does not riſe to that exceſs as in the heats of ſummer; and the waters in general are in a good condition, becauſe they have little evaporation, and the refreſhment of frequent ſhowers.

The earlier in ſpring a brewing is performed, the better. March is the next beſt month in the whole year to October; and, after this, as the weather grows warmer, it is leſs proper, becauſe

because it more approaches to the nature of summer.

As October is the best for the brown, this month succeeds the most happily of all others, with the pale low dried malt. This should be the great rule of difference between them, and the two brewings will mutually succeed the better.

CHAP. XXXIV.

Of the peculiar Virtue of well-cultivated Hops.

IF there be any thing wanting farther than these instructions fo the making the several kinds of beei in perfect excellence, it is the being secure of the high and full quality of the hop. The difference between *good* malt drink, and the *most excellent*, depends solely on the perfection of this ingredient. We have given rules for chusing the best among such as are offered to sale; but there is a

I 5 possibility

poſſibility of obtaining yet finer than any that are brought to market; for the quantity is more regarded than any thing elſe in thoſe which are raiſed for ſale.

No uſe of land is more beneficial than the planting it with hops; and we have an opportunity of giving the directions for raiſing them compleat, and from a very great and experienced hand. We ſhall add theſe at large: and whatever country-gentleman will follow them exactly, will not only ſupply himſelf with what are perfectly fine, but may diſpoſe of what he does not want at a great advantage.

CHAP. XXXV.

Of the Right Soil for Hops.

THE piece of ground ſelected for hops muſt be good, and deep in ſoil. No plant roots deeper than this, or requires more nouriſhment. A rich

A rich dusky mould, a fine black earth, or a very good loamy soil, are the only grounds wherein hops will grow well: nor will the best of these answer perfectly, unless there be also a proper bottom. Clay frequently lies under the soil; and, perhaps the most common bottom next to that is gravel; but neither of these are by any means proper for a hop-ground. The roots of this plant must be kept moist, but not wet; and the clay will hold too much water, and the gravel will let all through. Therefore these are both exceptions: the best bottom of all is a firm and pure loam; and this is very common, where the soil above is loamy: if all these things suit, there must also be depth of the good soil. If there be a full spade and a half depth, it will answer very well: less than this will not do; and if there be more, the better. There is a peculiar whitish land in Kent which has a great deal of marle naturally; and none ſucceeds better in hops than this. As for the others, the nearer they come to the nature of garden-mould, the better. The ſituation ſhould be ſuch as is defended from the North and North-eaſt by trees, buildings, or hills; it ſhould be open to the South-eaſt, and the more fully the wind can play about it, the better.

The ſpot being choſen, the next care muſt be to prepare the ground. The freſher the land is, the better the hops will grow; if the ſoil be equally good to the whole depth, very good plowing may anſwer the purpoſe of preparing it: but as it commonly happens, that the upper part is better than the lower, in this caſe it muſt be trenched by the ſpade, and the worſer part of the mould muſt be brought to the ſurface, where the weather will mellow and improve it; while the fineſt part, which before lay uppermoſt, is turned in to a depth, where the roots ſend their principal fibres. Great care muſt be taken, if, on on digging, the ground appears too wet. Drains muſt be cut, which muſt be kept carefully clean and open afterwards; and the ſoil in trenching muſt be thrown up in high ridges: it will, by this means, get rid of the abundant moiſture, and will be the more improved by the air. There are ſeveral kinds of hops which are ſuited to various little differences in the land, of which we ſhall ſpeak; but in whatever ſpot the hop-ground is fixed, the care ſhould be, that the land is not rendered uſeleſs afterwards: and there is great danger of this, if timely proviſion be not made by a right plantation. Hops will ſucceed very well upon the ſame piece of ground twelve or thirteen years; but, after this, a new ſpot ſhould be choſen for that crop; and if early care be not taken, the old one will be nearly uſeleſs. Hops exhauſt the ground ſo much in this long culture, that none of the com-

mon

mon crops will thrive upon it, whatever care be taken.

C H A P. XXXVI.

Of the Plantation of Trees among Hops.

THE beſt method is to provide by a plantation of uſeful trees, in Kent, where they have been long uſed to the culture of this plant. They make a double proviſion on this head; and that ſo judiciouſly, that their hop-grounds, while they yield a vaſt profit by the natural crop, are as ſo many nurſeries for their cherries and apples; in both which kinds they are alſo famous. The method is this, when they firſt lay out their hop-ground, they plant it with cherry and apple-trees: theſe do little hurt to the land; and they are excellently nouriſhed by the culture given it for the hop. When the ground is exhauſted by the hops, that

that is, at the end of ten, twelve, or fourteen years, according to the ſoil and management, the cherry-trees begin to bear; and the hops are removed to a new place. The cherries will bear very well a certain number of years; and in all that time the apple-trees will be only coming to their greateſt perfection: at the end of about five and twenty years, they grub up the cherry-trees; and after they have had ſeveral years the benefit of the apples the ground is fit for hops again; or for any other courſe of huſbandry. This is a proviſion for our children; but we ſhould remember how glad we are that our fathers have provided ſo for us.

CHAP. XXXVII.

Of the ſeveral Kinds of Hops.

ACcording to the nature of the ſoil, in thoſe ſmall differences we have named, the farmer is to fix upon

upon one or other of the kinds of hops; with theſe he is therefore to be ſeverally well acquainted for this purpoſe. In the hop countries they reckon four kinds, the wild garlick hop, the ſquare garlick, the long white hop, and the oval. The firſt of theſe is the wild hop of our hedges, the others have been raiſed from it by culture. They are vaſtly ſuperior to it in the produce, and there are peculiar ſoils which they ſeverally ſuit. The ſquare garlick has a redneſs about the ſtalk, which reduces the virtue; but it is a well-flavoured hop: there is a long garlick which differs a little from this in the length of the fruit; but is uſually reder than the ſquare. The oval hop is an excellent kind, pale-coloured, and of a good taſte. The long white is the beſt of all, it yields the fineſt hops of all; and in the greateſt quantity. This is always to be preferred, when the land will do for it. The wild hop is ſo much

much inferior to all the reſt, that it ſhould never be raiſed. The two others are to take their place, according as the ground may ſuit them. If the ſoil be poorer than one would wiſh for a hop-ground, the ſquare garlick is the kind to plant. For it is more of the nature of the wild hop than any of the others; and a good crop of this, which may be obtained upon middling ground, is better than a poor one of the others. In a middling ſoil the oval is to be raiſed for the ſame reaſon; but where the ground is perfectly good, no kind is to be thought of except the long white. This is always the kind for a pure and deep mould: when the ſoil is deep and moderately good, but has a tendency to be ſandy, the beſt way is to plant a mixture of the long white and oval, for they thrive very well together in ſuch ground. If, on the other hand, the ſoil is too tough, the long garlick muſt be the kind. Therefore, when the ground is is choſen, and the ſort or mixture of hop determined, the next care is to beſpeak a proper quantity of ſets to be ready for taking up at the time when the ground is got in order; and then to begin dreſſing it. The common practice is to plant the hops on hills, at ſuch diſtance, that a breaſt-plough can be conveniently uſed to work the ground between them. But of all the plants raiſed by the huſbandman, there is none that is ſo proper for the horſe-hoeing method; and, if they be planted for this purpoſe, there will be a farther advantage, which is, that being more diſtant than in the uſual way, the air will have a free courſe among them; and they will, by that means, be preſerved from moſt of thoſe accidents which are ſaid to render hops a precarious crop.

CHAP.

CHAP. XXXVIII.

The Preparation of the Ground.

IN the beginning of September, let the ground be ploughed up deep, or trenched, according to the nature and qualities of the ſoil; and after lying near a month in ridges, let the whole ſurface be laid ſmooth and level, by good harrowing. This will break the ſmall clods; and the ground being quite plain and uniform, is ready to be laid out for planting. The beſt diſtance for the hills is eight feet; therefore let a gardener's line be drawn acroſs the ground, at about a yard and half from one of the edges; and let a perſon go over the ground along it, with an eight-foot rod, and a number of ſmall ſticks. At every eight foot he is to ſtick up one of the ſticks; and when he has gone the length of the line, he is to move it eight

eight foot into the ground, and plant ſticks at every eight foot again. When he has gone over the whole land in this manner, the ſticks will ſhew where the hills are to ſtand; and, unleſs the ground be naturally very rich indeed, it will be proper to improve it in thoſe places by ſome manure. For this purpoſe, mix together four loads of fine rich mould, from under the turff of a good paſture; one load of very fine old and well rotted dung, and half a load of coarſe river-ſand. Turn theſe ſeveral times, and let the heap lie ready. Then at every place marked by a ſtick, open a hole with a ſpade, two foot deep and two foot wide; throw out the natural mould, and fill it up with a compoſt made of fine mould, river-mud, and cow-dung, that has been well-rooted. The holes being thus filled, the foundation of the ſeveral hills is laid; and the next care is planting: the ſets

the

being beſpoke, they are now to be taken up, the ground being got in this readineſs by the middle of October. The ſtrongeſt and healthieſt ſets are thoſe to be choſen; and the beſt choice falls upon the higheſt hills in the grounds from whence they are to be taken: thoſe alſo are always beſt which come from the hills that have produced the greateſt quantity. When theſe hills are opened to take out the ſets, care muſt be taken to get them out without injuring any part of them; and only the moſt perfect muſt be taken for the new ground; they ſhould be ten inches long, hearty in their growth, and they ſhould have four joints. As many ſhould be taken up as can be planted in the new ground the ſame day; or, if they are to be carried to a diſtance, the whole may be taken up at once. In this caſe, they muſt be laid in the ground, in a ſhady place, and only taken up as they are wanted

wanted by thoſe who plant them. Six of theſe ſets are to be planted in every hill; but, for this purpoſe, a hole of a ſpade deep, and above a foot broad, muſt be opened in the middle of each parcel of the manure; where the ſticks ſtood. The ſix ſets muſt be planted at equal diſtances round the hole, laying them up againſt the ſides, and placing them ſo, that the tops may be juſt upon a level with the ſurface of the ground. Then carefully pour in the mould that was thrown up in opening the hole, and fix it well with the hand about the ſeveral ſets, keeping them upright, and well ſurrounded with the pure mould. Then draw up a covering, of two inches, of the fine mould, over the tops of the ſets. This finiſhes the hole, and gives the firſt riſe of the hill in its place, which is thus about a finger's length higher than the ſurface of the ground. If the ſets are all got into the ground by the third week in October,

tober, there will be a good produce the firſt ſummer. Some plant the ground in ſpring, and then the plants are not ſtrong enough to bear that year: ſo they looſe the produce of one ſeaſon. In planting the ſets, if any one be injured by bruiſing, or any other way, it ſhould be thrown away: the value is but ſmall, and the miſchief would be great. The injured parts grow mouldy as ſoon as they are planted in the ground; and they not only decay themſelves, but infect the others.

CHAP. XXXIX.

Of the Planting the Sets.

THE whole ground having been prepared, by ploughing or trenching, nothing more will be needful, now the plantation is over, till the ſucceeding ſpring. The ſets will grow freely with the rains of autumn; and the depth at which they

they are planted, will ſufficiently preſerve them againſt froſt. The ground is to be thus left to itſelf all winter; but in ſpring it requires a thorough dreſſing, partly to deſtroy the weeds, and partly to give new nouriſhment to the crop. The common way is paring the ſurface with a ſpade, or with a breaſt-plough; but it will be much better to do it by ploughing up the intervals with the horſe-hoe. This ſhould be done in the beginning of April; and all that is required, is to break the ground very thoroughly. The plants in the hills will grow with a great deal of vigour after this; and the poles for tying them ſhould be fixed in the ground ſoon after. Five poles ſhould in general be allowed to each hill; and theſe, for the firſt year, ſhould not be nearly ſo tall as thoſe uſed afterwards: for the height of poles encourages the hop to grow in length, and this ſhould not be too much indulged the firſt ſeaſon. About four ſour thouſand poles will be required for every acre of hop-ground. Theſe for the firſt year, ſhould be about thirteen foot in length, and five inches and a half round: in the ſucceeding years, poles of five and twenty foot long, and ſeven inches and a half round, may be uſed. The moſt commodious method is to lay down the poles among hills, that they may be ready to ſtick up when they are wanted. They ſhould be ſharpened at the bottom, and always cut ſo as to have a fork at the top, either by a natural diviſion of the growth, or one of the ſide-branches may be cut ſo as to anſwer this purpoſe: it is of eſpecial ſervice; for the hop lies over the pole in the fork, and hangs down without pulling the reſt from the pole. The ſhort poles may be of alder; thoſe for the ſucceeding years ſhould be of ground-aſh, becauſe they will be tough enough to eſcape breaking with the wind, which has great ef-

K feƈt

fect upon them at that height, with the thick covering of the hop.

CHAP. XL.

Of fixing the Poles in the Ground.

THE poles lying ready, muſt be thruſt firmly into the ground, when the young ſhoots of the hop are about four inches long. They are to be thruſt firmly into the ground, at equal diſtances round about each hill, and fixed ſo well, that they will ſooner break than riſe. They ſhould ſtand nearly, but not exactly, upright; for the tops ſhould turn a very little outwards: this throws the long ſhoots of the hop naturally off from the hill; whereas if the tops of the poles bent ever ſo little inward, the hills would be covered by ſo many arbours, and the plants would be ſubject to many diſeaſes, for want of a due courſe of air. When a pole bends a little outwards,

wards, the hops will be produced in great plenty and perfection; because the sun has free access to the plant; but too much leaning will subject them to fall; neither, if they keep up, will they bear so well. When the poles are all up, the hops will of themselves, in most cases, lean to them; but in this they must soon after be assisted. When the shoots have got to be two feet and a half high, the poles should be looked over, to see if they be all firm, and stand right. Where any thing is amiss, the use of a heavy rammer forcing the earth about them, will drive them a little any way that should be thought proper, and they will afterwards keep their position. At the same time that this is done, the plants may be led to the poles and tied; the stalk of the hop must be wound twice round the pole, according to the motion of the sun. This is an essential article, for the growth will otherways be greatly disturbed. If we regard the wild hop in its climbing, we ſhall always ſee the round is made this way; and, as it is the natural effect of the heat forcing the growth principally that way, it would be very abſurd to attempt to put nature out of her courſe. When the hop is properly led round the pole, it muſt be kept in the place, by tying once near the ground, and once a little higher. Any thing that is ſoft will ſerve for tying them; but the propereſt thing of all is coarſe yarn, becauſe that is tender and capable of giving way. The hops muſt not be preſſed againſt the pole, only drawn towards it; if the ſtalks are brittle, as they are apt to be in rich ground, they muſt be tied about three of the clock in the afternoon, or from two to five; for, at that time of the day, the ſtems are tougher than at any other.

From this time the hops will grow very faſt, and will wind themſelves round the reſt of the poles, ſo that there

there needs no more trouble. Toward the middle of April they will be ſeven or eight feet high; and as ſome may now grow amiſs, they muſt be put right with a forked ſtick. They will eaſily take their proper form again, and after that time grow to the poles as well as at firſt. Toward the latter end of May the hops will be got up as high as the tops of theſe poles; and once more a labourer ſhould look to thoſe which do not grow kindly, laying the main ſtem over the fork of the pole. He muſt take a ſtep-ladder for this purpoſe; and this is the laſt care: for afterwards they will do perfectly well of themſelves. The time now is come for a ſecond horſe-hoeing; and as no more trouble is needful for the plant, there is natural leiſure to do it. If the ground had been broke ſooner the growth of the hop in ſtalk would have been promoted by it, which is by no means proper at that ſeaſon. We ſee the plants growing

K 3 very

very faſt without any ſuch aſſiſtance, and what we are to fear, is the carrying them up too high, becauſe the produce in fruit will be the leſs for it. Towards the end of May, the plants being got over the tops of the poles, have no more that inducement to riſe; and therefore what we give in nouriſhment by horſe-hoeing, goes towards the forming of the fruit, the firſt buds toward which are now made, though not yet viſible. In the common managament of a hop-ground, the beginning of June is the time when they pare the ſurface, to deſtroy the weeds and raiſe the hills: they take it off about an inch and a half deep in all the ſpace between hill and hill, and throw it up to the hills to raiſe them. This is a very imperfect method of dreſſing the ground; the horſe-hoe anſwering the purpoſe vaſtly better: and the making the hills up is ſtill eaſier, after the ſoil is thus broken; and the earth, which has been mouldered

mouldered to pieces by that inſtrument, gives much more ſtrength to the plants than the hard ſurface juſt pared away for that purpoſe.

CHAP. XLI.

Of Cleaning the Ground.

WHichever of theſe methods the planter chuſes, he ſhould firſt clean the hills; pulling up all weeds, and taking off the ſtraggling ſhoots of the hops themſelves, which only exhauſt the root, and are uſeleſs. After this, the earth turn'd up by the horſe-hoe ſhould be broke finer on the ſurface with the back of a ſpade; and then as much of it as is needful ſhould be thrown in upon the hills between, and all about the ſhoots of the hop plants. The hills ſhould be raiſed about four inches this time, and they ſhould ſpread proportionally at the bottom. Toward the end of June, they ſhould be raiſed once again by paring off ſome of the beſt of the mould in the intervals, and throwing on them; and when the hops begin to fill in July, the ground ſhould be once again horſe-hoed, and the hills made up again. If the horſe-hoe is not uſed, the ſurface muſt be pared by hand, and the hills raiſed at the ſame ſeaſons.

The firſt of theſe horſe-hoeings, or parings, which will be in the beginning of June, will give them new vigour; and, when this has very well fill'd the plant, and vegetation is ſtrong in it, after a little more growth, it muſt be turned to the branching of the plants, by ſtopping their perpendicular growth. The latter end of June is the right time for this, and it will be beſt effected by taking off the leading bud at the extremity of each plant: a careful perſon ſhould be ſent into the ground for this purpoſe with a ſtep-ladder; and this being ſet up againſt every hill, the plants are to be thus managed.

Such

Such as begin to branch, need not have the top taken off, but it ſhould be turned away from the pole; after which the ſtem will not encreaſe in length, but the tendency to branching will encreaſe: in all the others, which grow in length, and have no branches, the top of the plant muſt be pinched off with the finger and thumb; and after that there will be no more growth in length, but all the force of nature will be ſent to the branches, which will begin to form themſelves in a very few days from this ſtopping the ſhoot in length.

CHAP. XLII.

Of managing the Luxuriant Growth.

IN common ſeaſons thus much is all that is required; but ſometimes in wet years, and very rich grounds, the very branches will grow luxuriant in length, and the plant extending itſelf in bigneſs, will bear little fruit if this be not prevented. The ſame method anſwers the purpoſe perfectly. When theſe branches grow too long, their ends muſt be pinched off: the whole plant will then be covered with buds for fruit. We ſee this effect of taking off the luxuriant ſhoots in gardening, in a thouſand inſtances. Beans never bear ſo well as when their heads are pinched or cut off, and it will be found uſeful in many other caſes. The hop-ground is a garden of a particular kind, but all the garden rules hold good in it. After the pinching off the tops of the plants, the buds ſoon ſwell, and nature ripens them. The laſt horſe-hoeing is of prodigious ſervice in this reſpect; and hops ſo raiſed will exceed any that can be obtained by the common methods: the inferior kinds, with this management, will be equal to the beſt when they are leſs carefully raiſed; and the pooreſt grounds will receive moſt advantage by by it, which is a very happy incident. Where the planter uſes the horſe-hoeing method, he ſhould watch his time in the drieſt weather for performing it, becauſe the plow takes moſt effect, and works eaſieſt at thoſe ſeaſons; but when he is content with the old method of paring off by hand, the moſt favourable time is juſt after rain; becauſe the earth will not cut eaſily by the ſpade, or keep together at any other ſeaſons. There are many advantages in the horſe-hoeing method; but one of the greateſt is keeping the plants in health. Half the miſchief that happens in hop-grounds is owing to the want of a due ſupply of nouriſhment.

CHAP. XLIII.

Of Picking the Hops.

BY this management, the plants will flower in the latter end of July, and by the ſecond week in Auguſt the hops will form themſelves like bells. In the common way both theſe operations of nature will be a little later. Three weeks from their beginning to bell is required for ripening them; and, if the weather prove cold and rainy, it will be ſomewhat longer. Therefore from the end of Auguſt to the middle September, is the natural ſeaſon for gathering of hops. The hop till ripe is very moiſt and deſtitute of ſmell; when it begins to ripen, it grows dry, paler coloured, and fragrant. This is ſeen at a diſtance; but a more certain proof is obtained by examining the ſeeds. Theſe are at firſt green, and ſoft; but as they ripen they grow harder and brown: this is the perfect maturity of the hop, after which it ſoon looſes its fragrance, and falls to pieces if left upon the plant. The time of gathering the hop, is when they grow pale and dry, when they ſmell fragrant, and the ſeeds are juſt turned brown.

They

They are then perfect, and they must be pull'd immediately, for after this they will spoil every moment. The more hands there are in hop-grounds at the season, the better. The way is to cut off the plants a yard above the ground, and then to clear them at the top, by cutting the stalks with a sharp hook upon a long pole, where-ever they are entangled one with another. Thus every pole will be covered with its own plant, and free of all the rest; and it may then be pull'd up, and laid upon the ground for picking. The best management is to divide the hands into three or four parcels, and to make them begin in so many different parts of the ground. Four hills should be cut up first of all in each of these places, and a floor be prepared in the spot where they stood, by levelling the ground, and beating and rolling it. This serves as a place for the people to work upon; and the first hops they are to pick, should be those which grow upon the hills that were

were cut down for that purpoſe: after this the ground is to be cleared by degrees, in the ſame manner; carrying the plants, with their poles, to that floor which is neareſt the place. The ſafeſt way is to cut them down as faſt as they can be picked, and no faſter, for hops very eaſily get damage while they are upon the plant, after it is cut. The beſt way of taking up the poles, is by a lever and block; the lever being ſplit at one end in the manner of a pair of tongs, and that part lined and toothed with iron. The pole muſt be rocked about by the hand firſt; and then the block being laid over it, the ſplit end of the lever is to lay hold, and it will be torn up eaſily by bearing the lever down over the log.

The plants are not to be unwound, but carried, poles and, all to the next floor of picking; and the hops muſt be picked carefully and cleanly; none of them broken, nor no ſtalks left to them. The buyers of hops are very nice, and cleanlineſs and care make up a great a great article in their value. When the hop is full ripe, it loſes the heart in drying; but when gathered a little before that time, it has moſt virtue.

CHAP. XLIV.

Of Drying the Hops.

AS the fine colour and fragrance of hops are their great recommendation, there muſt be the utmoſt care taken to dry them quick, for this is the only way to preſerve both theſe characters. The quicker they are picked, the leſs damage they get upon the ſtalk; and after this they are to be carried directly to the kiln where they are dried. The great management is to proportion the ſeveral parts of the work one to another; to cut down the plants as faſt as they can be picked, and to pick them as faſt as they can be dried. If they are picked too faſt for the drying, they muſt be ſpread thin upon a floor, where there

is

is a thorough air, and turned now and then till there is room for them upon the kiln. A common malt kiln, with a hair-cloth for the hops, is the uſual method of drying, and ſucceeds very well; but there is a method practiſed in ſome places of a kiln, with a tin floor, and a kind of moveable roof, which anſwers much better; becauſe the roof reflecting the heat, dries the upper part of the hops, while the immediate heat of the floor dries the other; and thus the work is done without turning the hops; which is neceſſary in the other method; and which always does them more or leſs damage by breaking, and waſting the ſeeds. In Flanders they dry hops upon a kind of bed of rails, with ſmall ſpaces between, under which is a ſmooth floor, with a ſmall fire-place in the center. Charcoal is the beſt fuel; but in ſome places they burn wood, and the hops get a peculiar flavour by it. The hops may lie ſix inches thick upon this kind of kiln; and

and they muſt be moved a little where they dry floweſt, that all may dry alike. What feeds, and broken pieces of hops fall through theſe rails, muſt be ſwept together, and put to the reſt of the hops: but it is a much more delicate method to avoid breaking them or ſpilling the ſeeds at all, which may be contrived by the kind of kiln beforementioned; with a cover to let down or hold up as occaſion may require: the bed of tin may be laid upon a kind of lattice-work of wood; and upon this the hops may be laid ſeven inches thick, and they will dry thoroughly, and one of the ſides being made to fall down at pleaſure, by means of hinges. When the hops are dried, they may be thruſt off from that part without any danger of breaking, as there will be in any other way, becauſe they are moved to take them out while brittle from the drying. This is the time when they are moſt of all capable of injuries; becauſe the heat is yet in them:

them: they afterwards grow ſomewhat tough again in cooling.

CHAP. XLV.

Of Bagging the Hops.

WHEN the hops are taken from the kiln, they muſt be put in an airy room to grow gradually cold, and there to toughen: and thus they may be put up into bags and preſſed ever ſo hard without breaking. It will require three weeks, or longer, to give them this preparation. If they cool too faſt, there muſt be a blanket ſpread over them; and the ſame caution ſhould be uſed at times afterward, to aſſiſt the toughening of them if the weather is very dry. When they are ready for packing up, a hole is opened in the floor of the room which goes through the cieling. The meaſure of this ſhould be four foot by three, and a hoop is to be prepared that will not go through it, and that has a great deal

deal of ſtrength. The bag into which the hops are to be packed is to be faſtened to this hoop at its top, turning the edge all the way over the hoop, and ſowing it ſtrongly down with a packing needle: then the bag is to be put through the hole, the hoop keeping it from falling into the lower room. A few hops are to be thrown in and tied up in bundles at the corners; which will ſerve afterwards to handle and manage the bags; and when this is done, the reſt are to be thrown in by ſmall parcels at a time. A perſon gets into the bag to lay them well, and not only lays them even, but treads them down; all which violence they will now very well bear. When the bag is full the hoop is taken away, and it is ſown up at the top, leaving there alſo a couple of cuſhions at the corners; and thus the hops are ready for the market.

CHAP.

CHAP. XLVI.

Of Dressing the Ground.

THE ground requires no care all winter: the roots lie deep enough to be very safe from injuries by frost or accidents; and they will be strengthening themselves for the moist season. It is in the spring dressing of the hop-ground, that the planter will begin to perceive the advantage of the horse-hoeing husbandry: for if this method be followed, there will be no need of manure; but if he has managed the ground in the common way, and it has had no farther advantage than the paring away the surface, and making up the hills, there will be a necessity of a large quantity of manure. This is to be composed in the same manner as the compost for setting the roots, only with a double proportion of the dung; which must be very old, and well rotted, or else it it will deſtroy the crop. This manure ſhould be mixed up the autumn before, that it may lie to mellow together: and in ſpring the ſurface of the hop-ground is to be turned up with a common plow. The old ſtraw of the laſt year's hops ſhould be burnt upon the ground in ſeveral heaps, covered with a little of the mould; and this calcined earth and aſhes, together with the manure before directed, is to make up the hills for the next ſeaſon. The beginning of April is the beſt time for this work, for the hops ſhoot late, and the greateſt benefit will be obtained by dreſſing the hills a very little before the riſing of the buds.

The dreſſing of the hills muſt be done thus. The earth of the hill is to be drawn off, that the roots of the ſeveral plants may be ſeen. The old or original roots will at this time look of a freſh and glowing ruddy hue; theſe are to remain untouched: but the new roots, which are white, are in general to be cut away; only if any

any of them run downwards, thoſe are to be left on. The roots being thus dreſs'd, the ſhoots are to be managed much in the ſame manner. All the old or original ſhoots are to be left on; and if there be any new ones that riſe well, they are alſo to be left: but the generality of the new ſhoots are ill placed, and are to be taken off. This being the firſt dreſſing of the hills, the ſhoots muſt be taken off a finger's breadth from the old one; but in the following years they may be cut away cloſe.

CHAP. XLVII.

Of Selecting the beſt Plants.

IF any of the plants have the firſt ſummer yielded a bad hop, which is often the caſe, they ſhould be marked at the time by thruſting a ſtick down by them; and in this ſpring-dreſſing thoſe plants ſhould be taken entirely away, and ſome of the new ſhoots from the other hills ſet in their place.

When

When the roots and ſhoots are trimm'd, the hills are to be made up with the manure, and the earth taken from them to be ſpread in the intervals.

In the horſe-hoeing method all this trouble of new manure may be ſpared, for the whole earth of the intervals will be enriched by the frequent turning, and will itſelf ſerve as compoſt for the hills. In this method I ſhould adviſe, that, in the beginning of winter, the middle of the intervals throughout the whole ground ſhould be plowed up with the horſe-hoe; and thrown up high. In this way it ſhould lie all the winter, and the top of the ridge would then be mellowed by ſpring into a much better manure than any that could be procured from dung: for dung always hurts the hop when not ſufficiently rotted; and at beſt is not equal to ſuch a natural manure, as the proper ſoil, mellowed and enriched by the dews, froſts, ſnows, and thaws, of a whole winter.

In

In this cafe the hills fhould be taken down in April, and the roots and fhoots drefs'd exactly as in the foregoing directions; and then the tops of the ridges fhould be pared off with a fpade, and finally wrought up to the hills.

In this manner the fecond year's produce will greatly exceed the firft; and the third that of the fecond; and from that time the plants will continue in ftrength and vigour nine or ten years, if the ground be carefully drefs'd for them: but if at any time neglect has occafioned the plants to decline, the remedy muft be applying manure, fuch as defcribed before: if the ground has been cultivated the common way; but if by the horfe-hoeing hufbandry, there will need little more than deep plowing: if any manure has been given in the courfe of this method, it fhould be in the winter, between the third and fourth feafon; and again, in that between the eighth and ninth: and at thefe times a very fmall quantity will be fufficient, when a hop-ground that

that is cultivated in the ufual way, appears decaying, the fame roots will immediately grow ftrong, and flourifh, if planted in a new piece of land; and the horfe-hoeing hufbandry can give them the fame advantage while they ftand in their original ground. In the common way of management, the roots extend themfelves little farther than the fubftance of the hills, becaufe the ground of the intervals is too hard for their fibres to penetrate; but in the horfe-hoeing method, the whole ground is kept in a ftate of culture to a confiderable depth; and the roots, inftead of being confined to the hills for their nourifhment, fend fibres through the whole intervals. Every horfe-hoeing breaks off a multitude of thefe; and from every broken part arife numbers of others. So that the plants are from time to time furnifhed, not only with frefh nourifhment from the new-broken foil, but even with new mouths by which to receive it.

CHAP. XLVIII.

Of Watering a Hop-Ground.

A Vaſt advantage of the horſe-hoeing methods, is, that it always keeps the earth moiſt about the roots of the hops: for it is confirmed by all experience, that freſh-broken ground receives and detains the dews vaſtly more than ſuch as lies hard. In dry ſeaſons the planters are obliged to water the hop-grounds; and the extent of his plantations, and great quantity of water required for every hill, renders this a work of great expence. There never is any neceſſity for it in a hop-ground managed by the horſe-hoeing method. The ſeaſon, when drought, is thus prejudicial to the hops, is one of the times of the natural hoeings; and this never fails to ſupply nouriſhment as well as moiſture: it feeds the ſhoot as well as ſets it to growing. There are ſummers ſo dry

dry ſometimes, that two more waterings ſhall be neceſſary, one when the plants have obtained two thirds of their heighth, and the other juſt as they are preparing for flower and fruiting. Theſe alſo are two natural periods of the grounds being horſe-hoed; and thus in that excellent method, the whole goes on regularly, and even the moſt unfavourable ſeaſons loſe their ill effect.

CHAP. XLIX.

Of the Building for a Hop-Ground.

IF, on any account, one would wiſh the planter to add to the uſual expence of the ground, it would be to raiſe a large and coarſe ſhed, which would ſerve for picking the hops in ſafety at the ſeaſon: and in winter would preſerve the poles. This might be open on one ſide, and therefore conſiſting only of two ends, a back and a roof, might be built coarſely, yet ſtrongly, for a very moderate expence. The poles coſt a great deal, and are eaſily damaged in winter: whether they are laid along, or piled up endways. They give a great deal of trouble when they break; and there is a conſtant charge in new ſupplying the decayed ones. This would be all avoided by keeping them under cover; and a great deal of the expence of the ſhed would, in the courſe of time, be ſaved in this ſingle article. The planters very well know what damage the hops get by ſhowers of rain, or by a ſcorching ſun, while they lie for picking: and all this would be prevented by doing it under this ſlight cover: nor would there be that trouble and confuſion which always attends the picking hops in high-winds. It is ſaid, that in plantations where the hills are ſet at twelve or fourteen feet diſtance, the produce is as much from an acre, as when they ſtand cloſer; becauſe in this caſe the plants bear fruit all the way down; but at the diſtance here directed,

directed, the air has a free courſe, and the ſun full power; and more than this cannot be neceſſary. If the account given by Mr. Liſle, from the Wincheſter hop-merchant, be exact, it may be a rule for placing the hills ſomewhat more diſtant than here is ordered; but when he talks of double, he certainly means in reſpect to thoſe old plants when the hills were raiſed very cloſe, and the ground, for that reaſon, ſubject to frequent diſorders. It ſhould ſeem, that as the hop requires a moiſt earth about its roots, this very diſtant plantation, expoſing the ſurface too much, would hurt the crop in that reſpect. In all things moderation is the rule of wiſdom; and in the preſent inſtance it ſhould appear, that ſuch a diſtance between the hills, as is now directed, will anſwer the purpoſe of giving free paſſage to the air and ſun; which is all that can be propoſed on that head, when we conſider ſpaces of this extent; and yet will not expoſe the ſurface of the ground too much to the ſun. In the drying of hops, care ſhould be taken not to let them lie too long in the heat, for they will evaporate for ſome time after they are removed, from the heat that is ſtill left in them: and, if this be not allowed for in the kiln, they will be too dry. The fault of this is, that they never will acquire afterwards that ſoft damp and mellow condition which is perceived by the hand, in holding them; and is one of the great marks by which the buyers judge. There is a certain ſpirit in the hop beſide its bitterneſs, which it communicates to the beer; and this is loſt in too much drying. When this is gone, the hop has much leſs value; and cuſtom has taught them to judge of this by the ſoftneſs and dampneſs of it. Probably it never deceives them: but however that be, the planter will always find them depend a great deal upon this condition in the hop. Another rule of judging, is by the ſeed; therefore the planter muſt be be very careful not to loose this out of the hop in drying; nor to let them be gathered before they are of a due degree of maturity.

CHAP. L.

Of Cellarage.

WE shall raise the best hops, and brew the best liquor to little purpose, unless we know how to preserve it in perfection. This depends upon the method of keeping: and cellarage is the first article of all; for no care in the casks or bottles will be of any service, if the place where they are kept be faulty.

This article is very closely connected with the preceding; for certain cellars will spoil beers that are brewed at one time of the year, while they preserve and improve those which were brewed at another: thus, in general, cold and wet cellars will spoil beer brewed toward winter, be-

L 4 cause

cauſe they will check that fine and ſlow fermentation which mellows the drink in the caſk: and in the ſame manner, dry and warm cellars will ſpoil beer that was brewed in ſpring, by ſetting the fermentation too high.

Therefore he who would have good malt-liquors, muſt conſider every thing in time; and if he be to make a cellar, muſt chuſe a proper aſpect and condition of the ground: if, on the other hand, he is fixed in that particular, he muſt accommodate his ſeaſon to his cellar.

We have ſaid there are two ſeaſons particularly ſuited to brewing: theſe are autumn and ſpring; or, to name the time more diſtinctly, October and March. Theſe are nearly equal as to the advantage, and therefore one or other is to be choſen in regard to the difference of the cellar. As a cold damp cellar ſpoils beer in winter, and a warm dry one has the ſame ill effect in ſummer; and as it is beer newly brewed that ſuffers

ſuffers from this condition of the cellarage, if the brewer has a cellar upon a damp clayey ſoil, let him brew in March; and if on a dry gravel, let him brew in October: this would be taking the advantage of the particularity, which would otherwiſe have been hurtful: for the cold cellar will check the over fermentation of March beer, and the gravel cellar will promote the too languid fermentation of October.

When a cellar is to be made, the choice ſhould always fall upon a loamy ſoil, which is moderate as to the two extremes of heat and cold; and, in all cellars, the windows and door ſhould be to the weſt. The air has a great effect upon malt-liquors in the cellar, as well as the condition of the ground; and there are particular winds which foul the drink. Theſe ſhould be guarded againſt, as alſo all thoſe changes in the air which they occaſion. There is no occaſion for light in a cellar; therefore there

L 5 need

need be no windows; a candle will do all that is required in this place, and the doors may be guarded from the admiſſion of an improper air; though windows cannot.

A cellar ſhould always have a double door. There is a peculiar temper in the air of a cloſe cellar. And this agrees with drink: therefore we ſhould be careful how we alter it, by the admiſſion of that from abroad, eſpecially at improper ſeaſons. For this purpoſe it is we direct the double door, that there may be no current or paſſage for the common air immediately into the cellar. When the perſon goes in at the firſt door, he is to ſhut that upon himſelf, before he opens the other; and thus the cellar is defended. Some have been ſo cautious, as to have three doors, but two are fully ſufficient.

CHAP.

CHAP. LI.

Of Casks and Bungs.

THE cellar being prepared, the next care muſt be of the veſſels: and concerning theſe we have treated in general already; that they ſhould be of heart of oak, painted on the outſide (for that keeps their pores ſhut, and preſerves them and the drink) and as ſmooth as poſſible within; that there may be no lodgement for foulneſs in any crevices.

The bungs ſhould be of wood; for cork and clay are both hurtful. The beſt wood is poplar, becauſe it is very cleanly, void of taſte or ſcent; and has ſo much ſoftneſs, as to yield a little upon preſſure. They ſhould be made on purpoſe for the veſſel to which they are uſed; and turned by a good turner, to a perfect ſhape and ſmoothneſs. The beſt length is three inches and a half; and they ſhould

L 6 go

go about an inch, or ſomewhat more, into the caſk. The turner is to pierce them ſtrait through the center, length-wiſe, with a ſmall hole; and he muſt turn a peg to fit this hole.

Thus is the bung compleated; and, by means of the vent-hole, and its peg, there may at any time be a little air given, without opening the bung-hole: therefore, the bung ſhould be driven in very faſt, with a hammer, after the working; and it ſhould have a piece of clean cartridge-paper firſt wrapped round it, that it may fit in the cloſer.

When a new caſk is uſed, it ſhould be ſeaſoned twice with ſmall-beer, as has been before directed, before the fine ſtrong drink is put into it; and, in other caſes, it muſt always be prepared by a thorough cleaning, ſcalding with hot-water, and ſweetening in the air.

CHAP.

CHAP. LII.

Of Bottling.

THIS article we have alſo had occaſion to name ſlightly before, ſpeaking of the oat ale; but although what has been ſaid of that particular, be applicable alſo to others, there are ſome general rules to be obſerved beſide. In the firſt place, the bottles muſt be perfectly clean, and thoroughly drained. They ſhould ſtand in the racks draining two days; and it ſhould be in a place where there is a good, free air; becauſe they will there be ſweetened as well as drained.

The corks muſt be carefully picked, and none but the very even and ſoft kind, which they call the velvet-corks, muſt be uſed. There is nothing more diſagreeable than a cork's breaking in a bottle; which is the common caſe, where indifferent ones are

are uſed; and the difference in price is trifling, in compariſon of the ſatisfaction in uſing them. The very keeping of the beer alſo depends, in a great meaſure, upon due care in this article, for a coarſe cork does not ſtop like a ſoft and fine one; and, when they are very full of holes, air gets through. We expect the corks to ſtop cloſe; and we muſt chuſe the fineſt for that purpoſe. The evening before the beer is to be bottled, boil a quantity of water, enough to fill a waſh-tub, or ſome ſuch veſſel; pour it into the tub, and, when it has ſtood ten minutes, put in the corks, lay a board and a weight over them, to keep them down; and thus let them be till morning, then ſpread them to dry, before they are uſed. This ſoaking will make them a little pliable, and they will go in eaſier, and fit better to the bottles.

Three perſons ſhould be employed in bottling of beer; one to draw it from

from the caſk; another to cork the bottles; and a third to take them from the corker, and ſet them up. The cellar ſhould be ſhut up the whole time; and the work done by candle-light. The buſineſs is to get it quietly into the bottles; and any change in the air will bring on a new fermentation. 'Tis therefore the cellar is to be kept ſhut up: and as motion will take the ſame effect, in bringing on a working in the liquor, all poſſible care is to be taken to prevent it. The quicker and the quieter this buſineſs is performed, the better it ſucceeds; and three pair of hands aſſiſting in both theſe purpoſes, the beer may thus be drawn ſteadily, by a perſon who does nothing elſe; the bottles may be given, evenly and ſmoothly, from him to the corker. The corks being well choſen, and prepared by this ſoaking, will go in eaſily and freely; and, if the quantity be large, ſo that they muſt be carried to ſome diſtance,

distance, a fourth person may be employed, to hand them to their place. Thus they need be scarce a minute in any one person's hand to heat; nor be shook in moving, when there are persons enough to receive them. Some prefer laying the bottles on one side; and others turn them bottom upwards: but what we want, is to have the drink clear; and, if there be any little settlement, it is best at the bottom. Therefore the bottles should always stand upright.

CHAP. LIII.

Of Remedies for Faults in Malt-Liquors.

THE common brewers use many ingredients, beside those we have named, in making of their beers: and when they grow foul, or become stale, or otherways faulty, they have a long list of remedies to recover

recover them. Thoſe who will follow the directions here given, will need no other expedients than malt, hops, and water, to make the moſt excellent of malt-drinks; nor will they be apt to fail or become faulty: however, though we utterly diſcommend the uſe of jalap, ginger, treacle, and the like, in brewing; yet, as by ſome accident or over-ſight, the beſt brewer may ſometimes have his beer turn bad, we ſhall not omit the methods of prevention, when the danger is foreſeen; or the remedies that may be innocently and ſafely uſed, when it has happened.

As it is better to prevent the miſchief than to ſuffer it, and then try an uncertain remedy, we ſhall firſt give the way of preparing what is called the feeding-paſte: this is a compoſition, the ingredients of which are all innocent, and all tend to the ſame purpoſe; therefore it is effectual.

We

We know the brewers mean by food, ſomething that is to remain at the bottom of the caſk, and upon which the drink lies and mellows. Often the fineſt part of its natural ſediment anſwers this purpoſe; but when that is deficient, or more is required than will naturally reſult from its effect, the feeding-paſte is very proper. It is thus made.

Diſſolve two ounces of the fineſt iſinglaſs in as much good ſtrong-beer as will thoroughly melt it; then add to this a pound and half of good lump-ſugar. Let them ſtand till the ſugar alſo is melted. Powder very fine three pounds of clean ſoft chalk, and one pound of white oyſter-ſhells, ſuch as are ſold at the druggiſts; add to this, of the flour of malt, ſifted fine, one pound and a quarter, and powder of hops two ounces: grind theſe well together; then put in the ſyrup of iſinglaſs, and beat up the whole, in a marble mortar, to a good paſte; ſpread this upon a piece of paper,

paper, on the back of a large ſieve, and lay it in the air to dry. When it is hard and dry, put it up for uſe. Two pounds of this is the proper quantity to be put into a hogſhead of drink; and it muſt be uſed in a like proportion for any leſſer or greater quantity. If any ſmall over-ſight has happened in the brewing; or if the ſeaſon of the year has been unfavourable, or there be any other cauſe to fear the drink may grow ſour, or come to other harm; this, being put in at the faſtening down the bung, will prevent the miſchief. The beer will be fine, clear, ſoft and well-taſted; and will keep without danger.

If from any omiſſion of this aſſiſtance, when it was neceſſary, or from any other cauſe, a caſk of beer grows unexpectedly foul and thick, and taſtes, as it always will in that caſe, dead and muddy; the proper remedy is by a ſyrup of the hop, made with iſinglaſs. The way to prepare

prepare it is this: and for a hogſhead, the following quantity. Rub to pieces a pound of fine, freſh hops; put them into a ſtone jar, and pour upon them as much boiling water as will cover them, without preſſing them down: ſtop up the jar, and ſet it in a large pan of boiling water: pour away this as often as it cools, and put freſh boiling water in its place: in this manner keep the hops ſtewing, in the cloſe jar, twelve hours: then let them ſtand twelve hours longer in the cold. After this ſtrain the liquor, without preſſing the hops: diſſolve in this two ounces and a half of beaten iſinglaſs; and then, to every pint of the liquor, put a pound and half of lump-ſugar; boil this once up, to melt the ſugar, and ſtrain it through a flannel bag. When this is ready, clean and ſweeten a freſh caſk. Burn two or three brimſtone-matches in it; then put in this ſyrup: draw off the beer, out of the hogſhead it was in, carefully into

into this; and leave all the ſettlement behind. Bung it up, but leave the vent hole open a little, for three or four days; then ſtop it up entirely, and let it ſtand three weeks; after which it will be perfectly fine.

One farther accident there is attending beer, which it is eaſy to prevent, but very difficult to cure; and which is ſo general, that it requires great care to obviate: this is, the getting that ill taſte and quality which the brewers call the Fox. This is a roapyneſs of the beer, with an ill taſte, and diſagreeable ſmell. It will never be found in beers brewed with the care we have directed: for cleanlineſs has been one of the great points recommended here; and the want of that is uſually the cauſe of this miſchief. Some of the wort of a former brewing, is too often left in the crevices of the veſſels; which no ſcalding will then get out. They muſt be cleaned at firſt, or it can never be well done at all. A very

very ſmall quantity of this foulneſs will do the miſchief; for it inevitably grows ſour in the cracks; and, when the new wort comes into thoſe veſſels, this brings on a falſe fermentation, which prevents and interrupts the due operation of the other; and the beer, in the end, gets an ill taſte and ſmell from this matter and its foulneſs, from the want of a due fermentation. Perfect cleanlineſs will always prevent this; but the remedy is difficult: the following is the only one I have found ſucceed.

Grate half a pound of ſea-biſcuit fine, mix with it a quarter of a pound of very white wood-aſhes, and a pound of ſlaked-lime; mix this with a little of the beer, and put it to the reſt: then let it ſtand a fortnight. This quantity is ſufficient for a hogſhead; and I have ſeen it often ſucceed.

After this time of ſtanding, if upon a little of the beer being drawn out, the taſte is ſtill perceived, make a a new mixture of the ſame ingredients, with the addition of a ſmall quantity of the ſeed of hop, and it ſcarce ever fails.

For this purpoſe, ſome of the ſeed of hops that falls out in the drying, muſt be carefully ſaved in time: then burn ſome clean wood purpoſely to very white aſhes, and mix three ounces of theſe with nine ounces of lime, that has lain in the air till quite reduced to powder. Bruiſe an ounce and half of the hop ſeed in a marble mortar; and mix with theſe: then add the ſame quantity of biſcuit, and uſe this as the former. Let it ſtand a month, and it will probably be quite cured.

FINIS.

INDEX.

A.

B.

M Brew-

I N D E X.

C.

D.

Diſpo-

INDEX.

I.

K.

L.

M.

Maſhing,

INDEX.

Quantity

INDEX.

Q.

R.

S.

T.

U.

Water

INDEX.

W.

The Art
OF
MAKING AND MANAGING
CYDER.
&c. &c.

A New Edition.

PRICE ONE SHILLING.

THE ART OF MAKING AND MANAGING CYDER,

DEDUCED FROM

Rational Principles,

AND

ACTUAL EXPERIENCE.

By ABRAHAM CROCKER, M. S. A. &c.

.... "Cyder
"Shall please all Tastes, and triumph o'er the Vine."
Philips.

TAUNTON:
Printed for the Author, by J. Poole;
And sold by B. Crosby and Co. Stationers'-Court, London,
And by all Booksellers in the Country.
1806.

PREFACE.

THE Writer of the following pages, having lived the best part of his life in a Cyder country, and having, from a long series of observation on the practice of others, and from the result of his own procedure in the business of Cyder-Making, acquired a knowledge of the art, was some years since prevailed on to arrange the substance of that knowledge into a systematic form, and to communicate the same to a few particular Friends. Since which time he has had the satisfaction of observing, that those communications have been honoured with a place in the Transactions of the Philosophical Society in America, as well as in a very popular provincial Agricultural Survey in his own country.

A 3

Thus honoured with a tacit approbation of the principles he had laid down, he has been induced to enlarge his ideas on the subject, and to submit them to the public at large; under a hope, that his country may derive some advantage from such communication.

He has not the vanity to suppose, that the principles contained in the present publication, are unknown to all Cyderists; but he feels confident that many of his readers will meet with various useful hints therein, which have hitherto escaped their attention: and that, by such means the art of Cyder-making may in future be rendered more certain and perfect, and consequently become more advantageous to the community.

Frome, January 1st, 1806.

THE ART

OF

Making and Managing Cyder.

APPLES.

THE art and industry of mankind have, for some centuries past, been sedulously employed in procuring and propogating a variety of autumnal fruits in this country; but among them all, none is of such vast importance (taken in its various general uses and pleasurable advantages) as the Apple. The easy means by which it is procured; the varieties of its flavour; the aptitude of its keeping sound for many months longer than other fruits; and its applicability to the various uses of all degrees of mankind, from the cottager to the prince, proclaim it the most useful and valuable fruit which this kingdom produces.

A 4

The following pages will be principally directed to the consideration of its virtues in producing a wholesome, vinous beverage, which, when used with rational moderation, tends to lighten the cares of mankind, and to heighten their friendships.

As apples are the ground-work of cyder, and as the cultivation of the superior sorts, and the consequent exclusion of the inferior ones, may be of much future advantage to the public, it is presumed, that the introducing here a brief description of some of the better species thereof will stand in no need of an apology.

The orchardists of Herefordshire and Worcestershire have long been in the habit of propogating a variety of good cyder-fruits; among which the following seem to be the most valuable.

The *Red-streak.* An apple of small size, yellow about the pedicle, a light red-coloured ground about the upper part, thickly tinged with lake-coloured streaks, slightly spotted with red within, of a sharp acid flavour; makes very good cyder.

Hagloe Crab. Of a moderate size, yellow colour, sharp taste; makes good but not very rich cyder.

Old Quining. A large red apple, makes good cyder; but is getting out of use, as the tree is very subject to canker.

Bennet Apple. Streaked with red, of a pleasant taste, and makes a good second-rate cyder.

Capt. Nurse's Kernel. Yellow, streaked with red, of a mild acid flavour; makes light, pleasant cyder.

Elton's Yellow. Of this apple there are two sorts, the one to be met with *above* Hereford, and the other *below*; the former of the shape and size of an orange, yellow on one side and red on the other, of a mild, pleasant acid, and makes very good cyder; the latter is somewhat larger, and of a beautiful gold colour, sharp to the taste, and makes excellent cyder.

Normandy Apple. Under this name there are three sorts; the yellow, the white, and the green, all of a bitter-sweet

A 5

taste; which make rich cyder, of a high colour. The trees are said to be most abundant bearers.*

Pauson Apple. Large, of a yellowish green; makes a delicious cyder, of a beautiful colour.

Red Styre. Of a red colour, mild acid; makes good stout cyder.

Yellow or *Forest Styre.* Small, red on one side, and a fine yellow on the other, of a mild, pleasant acid; and, in the opinion of many, makes the most excellent cyder. The tree, however, seldom thrives well, and is but a shy bearer.

Somersetshire produces a great variety of cyder apples, of which the following ought to be held in the highest estimation.

The Jersey. Small, of a light red ground, with a variety of lake-coloured

---

* The writer hereof has been informed by a friend, whose veracity may be depended on, that thirty trees of this sort, in the fifth year after grafting, produced five hogsheads of cyder of 110 gallons each.

streaks, moderately bitter; makes high-coloured cyder, which is sluggish in its fermentation, and particularly ought to be made by itself.

White-Sour. Small, of a yellow ground lightly tinged towards the nose with a light brown, and some strong touches of brown near the stem; of an acid flavour, somewhat acrid, very juicy; and makes smart, palatable cyder.

Margill. Middle-sized, yellow lightly tinged with red, pleasant flavour; is a fine cyder fruit.

Vallis Apple. Large and handsome, finely tinged with red all over, sweet in its flavour, very juicy; makes tolerable cyder.

Barn's-Door. Moderate size, brown towards the stem, the rest part red, some red streaks within, late in ripening, a pleasant acid; makes very good cyder.

Crab Red-streak. Small, greenish yellow on one side, light red on the other, with strong red streaks, of a pungent acid; and, under proper management, makes smart stout cyder.

Du-ann. Small, yellow near the stem, strongly tinged with red towards the nose, smart acid; makes good cyder.

Jack Every. Middle size, light yellow tinged with brown and red, sweet flavour; makes tolerable cyder.

Cockagee. Yellow, spotted with red and brown, of a rough acrid flavour; makes very smart cyder under due management; but its fermentation being particularly volatile, it requires much attention soon after making.

Clark's Primo. Middle size, of an orange colour on one side, red blotched with brown on the other, of a mild luscious acid; makes rich cyder, and is also an excellent apple for the table.

Buckland. Small, yellow tinged with red, veined with red within; makes good cyder.

Pit-Crab. Small, dark red finely tinged with a lake colour within, smart acid; makes good cyder.

Slatter's Pearmain. Middle-size, yellow richly tinged with red and brown, delicious flavour, firm flesh; makes excellent cyder, but hitherto has been more used at the table than at the press.

Slatter's No. 19. Long in its form, ground a yellow and light red, finely blotched with strong red, moderately acrid; is a fine cyder fruit.

Slatter's No. 20. Yellowish ground tinged with red, small acid flavour; makes very good cyder.

Slatter's No. 21. Tinged on the sun side with red and brown, very pleasant flavour; and will undoubtedly be esteemed as one of our best cyder-apples.*

Castle-Pippin. Greenish yellow, veined with brown, and slightly tinged with red, a mild acid; and makes good second-rate pale cyder.

* The four last-named apples are new, the trees being lately raised from kernels by the gentleman whose name they bear, (Mr. Slatter of Ilminster, Somerset) and whose orchards and cyder have long acquired a celebrity which others are not entitled to.

Saw-pit. Red throughout, acid flavour; and by some is esteemed the best cyder-apple in the country.

Pomme Apis. Large, yellow, faintly tinged with red on the sun side, broad at the stem, very juicy, smart but pleasant acid; is undoubtedly a fine cyder-fruit.*

Devonshire possesses many very valuable species of cyder-apples, from which the following are selected, as being the most celebrious:

Staverton Red-streak. Whitish yellow at the stem, brown tinged with red towards the upper end, pungent acid; makes a smart but pale-coloured cyder. The tree a remarkably plentiful bearer.

Sweet Broady. Large and handsome, colour brown and red; makes good cyder, useful for mellowing that of the very

---

* This apple is very little known in this country, having been brought from France but a few years, and the propagation thereof being confined to one or two nurseries only.

acid fruits. The tree large and fine, and bears plentifully.

Lemon Bitter-Sweet. Yellow rind, hard and firm, a pleasant bitter, and is by some esteemed a fine cyder-apple.

Josey. A handsome yellow, subject to spots of brown on the rind, of a mild acid taste, very soon after gathering perfects the saccharine fermentation; makes mild pleasant cyder, but not lasting. It is also a good table-fruit.

Orcheton Pippin. A very handsome apple, yellow on one side and red on the other; of a highly-pleasant flavour, excellent for cyder, the table, and the kitchen; in point of general utility, perhaps, few apples are superior.

Wine Apple. Greenish yellow ground, very thickly streaked with red all over, pulp a little red, mild acid; is a very good cyder-fruit.

Marygold Spice Apple. Yellow ground, light brown about the stem, highly and beautifully tinged with pink, mild acid, of a spicy relish; makes excellent cyder of a delicious flavour: it is a delicate fruit also for the table, and keeps long.

Ludbrook Red-streak. Yellow ground finely tinged with pink, smart acid; and makes excellent cyder. The tree subject to canker.

Green Cornish. Yellow with green ground lightly tinged with red, of a mild acid flavour, early ripe; and makes good cyder.

Butter-Box. Yellowish green tinged with light red, mild acid; makes pleasant, but not lasting cyder.

Red Cornish. Red nearly all over, of a mild acid; makes good cyder.

Broad-nosed Pippin. Large, rich yellow, mild acid; makes pleasant, but not strong cyder.

Cat's Head. Large, greenish yellow, pleasant acid; makes good cyder.

Brandy Apple. Middling size, white, smart acid; makes pale-coloured frisky cyder.

Pine's Red-streak. Very handsome, red all over except at the stem, flavour not so smart as the *Ludbrook;* but makes a cyder equally good.

Winter-Red. Dark red with some tinges of brown at the stem, crisp in its pulp, very juicy, of a smart spicy flavour, will keep until April, and is excellent both for cyder and the table.

Sweet Pomme-Roi. Yellowish green on the shade-side, and brown tinged with red on the sun-side, of a luscious flavour; is deemed a good cyder-apple.

Bickley Red-streak. A late fruit, greenish and yellow finely tinged with red, pulp firm, flavour somewhat acrid; is a most excellent cyder-apple.

Although the sorts of apples above described deserve particular commendation as cyder-fruit, yet there are many others in each of the cyder counties, from which, under due management, not only tolerable, but good cyder might be made; but from the foregoing catalogue any nurseryman will find ample choice to propagate from, in future.

It cannot but be observed, that names are given to apples arbitrarily, and which are by no means fully expressive of their qualities; but if there be a general characteristic of good cyder-fruit, it seems to be this:—that the apple which is of a yellow or light-red ground, tinged with red-streaks on the sun side; of a smart acid flavour; with firm but juicy parenchyma, and of an aromatic flavour; be it called by what name soever it may, will doubtlessly make good cyder.

It has been remarked by a writer of the present day, (—— Knight, Esq;) that the properties which constitute a good apple for cyder and the dessert, are seldom found in the same fruit.—The firmness of pulp which is essential in an eating-apple is useless in the cyder-fruit: and colour, which is disregarded in the former, is amongst the first qualities of the latter: some degree of astringency, which is injurious to the eating fruit, is advantageous to the other.

GATHERING APPLES.

Apples should be thoroughly ripe ere they are taken from the tree, otherwise the cyder will be of a rough, harsh taste, in spite of all endeavours.

The most certain indications of the ripeness of apples is the fragrance of their smell, and their spontaneously dropping from the trees. When they are in this state of maturity, in a dry day, the limbs may be slightly shaken, and partly disburthened of their golden store; thus taking such apples only as are ripe, and leaving the unripe longer on the trees, that they may also acquire a due degree of maturity. It may not be amiss to make three gatherings of the crop, keeping each by itself. The latter gathering (as well as windfalls) can only be employed in making inferior cyder: the prime cyder will be drawn from the former gatherings.

That cyderist who would be particularly curious in his prime liquor, will doubtlessly hand-gather his fruit, and keep the sorts separate one from another; but as this would be troublesome, expensive, and in a full season wholly impracticable, the general crop may, at different times, be shaken down, and collected from the ground.

Fruit of equal ripeness, and whose qualities are nearly alike, may be heaped together, to meliorate their juices, or, in other words, to perfect the saccharine fermentation.—How this is best done, cyder makers are not agreed: some judging it altogether unnecessary to heap them at all, if sufficient time be allowed for perfecting the saccharine fermentation on the tree:—some considering it best to sweat them in close lofts:—whilst others alledge, that the open air is the only place where they ought to be heaped.

Experience, however, should teach us, that most apples require time for their being mellowed, to attain their highest flavour; and until this mellowing be perfected, their juices are not in the best state for being converted to cyder.

Philosophers well know, that fermentation is never improved by hastening the operation with too much heat; nor perfected in due time under too great an exposure to cold. It would be well, therefore, if apples, when gathered from the tree, were placed in open sheds, having boarded floors, in heaps or layers, of ten or twelve inches deep;* the sorts to be kept separate, as much as the conveniences of the sheds will allow:—at any rate, if there must be a mixture of apples in the same heap, let them be such as are of qualities nearly alike, and which are of equal ripeness at the time of gathering, but on no account should sweet and sour be heaped together. To some cyderists it might have appeared unnecessary to keep the different sorts of apples sepa-

* The hard and harsh fruits may be lain in heaps of greater depth.

rate; but it is of importance so to do; and the trouble thereof is very little, compared to the advantages which will hereafter result from a regular fermentation of the juices.

Surely, the impropriety of housing and laying apples in very large heaps must be manifest to every thinking mind; more especially when in the same room are found all sorts; sweet, sour, harsh, generous, ripe, and unripe, thrown promiscuously together, where some are rotten ere others are mellowed.—And what must the liquor be which is expressed from such an heterogeneous mass?

But let us now suppose, that the fruit, which is of different sorts and qualities, has been kept separate from one another a few weeks; it will be perceived, that some of the prime sorts are in a proper state of maturation; that the pulp has acquired its highest degree of richness; the kernels assumed their brownest colour; the rind still free from any appearance of rottenness; and that they readily yield to the pressure of the thumb;—then is the time, and such is the fruit to be employed in making prime cyder:—Every necessary utensil must now be set in order: the mill, press, tubs, casks, pails and bowls, clean washed, and suffered to dry before they are used.

GRINDING, ETC.

SEVERAL methods are practised for converting apples to pommage; but the two most chiefly in use are, the bruising-stone with a circular trough, and the apple-mill. In the trough, the apples are thrown and bruised by the motion of the stone, as it is moved round by a horse, in the way that tanners grind bark. This is an ancient method, and still in use in some parts of Devonshire; and although it has its inconveniences, in bruising some apples too much and some too little, it is not without its advocates in those parts.

of the country; who alledge, that it bruises the kernels of the fruit better than other machines. Although it must be admitted, that the kernels possess an agreeable aromatic bitter, yet it has been held questionable if they impart any perceivable beneficial quality to the cyder. Be this as it may, certain it is, that this method of converting apples to pommage by the trough and stone has, in the last fifty years, much given way to the *Apple-mill.*

Of this latter machine there are various constructions; some being worked by hand, some by horses and others by water. Whichever of the powers be employed, the best internal construction of a mill seems to be that which has two pair of rollers; the upper part being stuck with *coggs* and *dags*, and the under pair, being of very hard wood, turned smooth, and worked with coggs only. The upper rollers grinding the apples to a coarse pommage, and the under ones squeezing it to what it ought to be—a very fine pulp.

There are also *Cyder-presses* of various constructions; some being compounded of a bed, and heavy cumbrous piece of timber called a *summer*, which is generally worked with a lever and capstain. Others, instead of the summer, are constructed with a single, but large, wood screw. This construction has for some years been superseded by another sort, which has two iron screws, like that which cloth-workers use in pressing cloth. There is also another, of modern construction, superior to the others, which works a summer-piece by means of a winch and cast-iron wheels and pinions. This construction is yet little in use; but it is not unlikely, that when it is generally known, that one hand at the winch will give a sufficient pressure to a a cyder-cheese, it will be particularly sought after.

Cyderists have not agreed in opinion, whether the pommage should immediately after grinding be conveyed to the press, there to be formed into what is

B

called the *cheese*; or whether it should remain some time in that state before pressing. Some say it should be pressed immediately after grinding; others conceive it best to suffer it to remain in the grinding trough, or in vats employed for that purpose, for twenty-four hours, or even two days, that it may acquire not only a redness of colour, but also that it may form an extract with the rind and kernels. Both extremes are wrong.

There is an analogy between the making of cyder from apples, and wine from grapes: and the method which the wine-maker pursues, ought to be followed by the cyder-maker. When the pulp of the grapes has lain some time in the vats, the vintager thrusts his hand into the pulp, and takes some from the middle of the mass; and when he perceives, by the smell, that the luscious sweetness is gone off, and that his nose is affected with a slight piquancy, he immediately carries it to the press, and by a light pressure expresses his prime juice. In like manner should the Cyderist determine the time when his pulp should be carried to the press. If he carry it thither immediately from the mill to the press, he might lose some small advantage which may be expected from the rinds and kernels, and his liquor may be of lower colour than he might wish. If he suffer it to remain too long unpressed, he will find, to his cost, that the acetous fermentation (hereafter to be spoken of) will come on, before the vinous is perfected; especially in the early part of the cyder-making season. He will generally find that his pulp is in a fit state for pressing in about twelve or sixteen hours. If he must, of necessity, keep it in that state longer, he will find a sensible heat therein, which will engender a premature fermentation; and he must not delay turning it over, thereby to expose the middle of the mass to the influence of the atmosphere.

The pommage being now in a proper state, it is carried to the press, and a square cheese made thereof, by placing

B 2

very clean sweet straw or reed between the various layers of pommage; or else by putting the same into hair-cloths, and placing them one on another.* To this cheese, after standing awhile, a slight pressure is at first to be given, which must be gradually increased, until all the *must* or juice is expressed:—after which this juice must be strained through a coarse hair sieve, to keep back the gross feculencies of the juice, and be put into proper vessels.

These vessels may be either open vats or close casks; but as, in the time of a plentiful crop of apples, a number of open vats may by the Cyderist be considered an incumbrance in his cyder-rooms, the *must* is generally carried immediately from the press to the cask.

* It is of importance, that the straw or reed be sweet and perfectly free from any fustiness, lest the cyder be impregnated therewith.—Particular care ought also to be taken to keep hair-cloths sweet, by frequently washing and drying; else the ill effects of their acidity will be communicated to the cyder.

Thus far cyder-making is a mere manual operation, performed with very little skill in the operator; but now it is when the great art of making *good cyder* commences:—Nature soon begins to work a wonderful change in this foul-looking, turbid, fulsome, and unwholesome fluid; and, by the single process of *fermentation* alone, converts it into a wholesome vinous, salubrious, heart-cheering beverage.

FERMENTATION.

PHILOSOPHERS inform us, and experience justifies the position, that the juices of all vegetables, when exposed to certain degrees of heat and atmospheric influence, are disposed by nature to a spontaneous intestine motion of their constituent parts:—this intestine motion is called *fermentation.*

This principle is, in a thousand instances, evident to the senses; yet the first cause, or original source thereof, the human understanding has as imperfect a conception of, as it has of attraction or any other of the arcana of nature, which are to remain among the mysteries of created matter to the end of time.—Yet from what we know of it, by its effects, we may derive no small advantage to ourselves, if we duly attend to the regular operations thereof.

Cyder, and all other fermentable liquors, in the precise chemical notion of them, consist of saline, mucilagenous, and oleagenous matter, diluted with a large portion of water:—by the water the other parts are set at a distance from one another; the saline ones are interspersed among the subtle earthy ones, which make the slimeness; and they, together, imbibe, detain, entangle, and attract the grosser oily parts: besides which, there are oily parts still more subtle, that by means of the highly-attenuated saline portion adhering to them, remain as much connected with the water as the rest: and these are what are called the spirituous part. The action and essence of fermentation is a separation and destruction of the former connexion of these principles in the fermenting subject, and the transposing them anew.

It is well known, that there are various stages of fermentation in the juices of all vegetables, each of which changes the very nature and quality of the fluid; but the principal which are to be particularly attended to, in the instance now under consideration, (the *must*, or juice of apples) are three; namely, the *vinous*, the *acetous*, and the *putrefactive*. The first converts the *must* from its turbid, fulsome state, to a transparent spirituous liquor, lightly piquant on the palate, resembling wine both in its flavour and effects. If the juice be expressed from *sour* apples, this fermentation is perfected in two or three days; but if from *sweet* apples, not under a week or ten days, or longer.—The next stage of fermentation gives an acidity to the vinous liquor be-

B 4

fore spoken of, converting it to a sort of vinegar. This fermentation begins soon (frequently in a few hours) after the vinous is ended; and if the fermentation be improperly hastened by heat, *before* the vinous can be perfected.—The third (and all succeeding fermentations) disengages an alkali from the liquor, and gives it a tendency to putrefaction.

Although we cannot form any clear and distinct knowledge of the precise manner in which nature performs these changes in fermenting liquors, yet the effects are evident; and from a consideration of the different natures and effects of the various fermentations, it may be perceived, that the *first* is the only one useful in making good cyder; and that the others tend to vitiate, and render unwholesome, a liquor that otherwise would be highly pleasant and truly salubrious. To regulate the first, and to check the others, is then the great business of that cyder-maker, who would attach to himself the satisfaction and fame which every one is emulous of.—Let us therefore consider how these ends are best attained.

Fermentations should not, by too much heat, be carried on rapidly; nor, by extreme cold, too slowly; as in each case the fermenting body will be injured.*—Hence it appears, that a certain degree of warmth, or rather imperceptible heat, conduces best to regulate this operation. This degree of warmth may be understood to rest between forty and fifty degrees of FARENHEIT's thermometer. If then the warmth of the cellar, in which new-made cyder is placed, be between these points, (no adventitious cause intervening), we may expect that the vinous fermentation will commence and go on with due regularity.

It has been observed above, that fermentation is an intestine motion of the

* Too great heat, says STAHL, is the bane of all vinous fermentation, and extreme cold represses it :—and MACQUER tells us, that if fermentation be slow and tedious, the liquor cannot be good.

B 5

parts of a fermentable body:—this motion in the present case, is always accompanied with an evident ebullition; the bubbles rising to the surface, and, there forming a scum, or soft and spongy crust over the whole liquor. This crust is frequently raised and broken by the air as it disengages itself from the liquor, and forces its way through it. This effect continues whilst the fermentation is brisk, but at last gradually ceases: the liquor now appears tolerably clear to the eye; and has a piquant vinous sharpness upon the tongue.*

Now is the critical moment which the cyderist must not lose sight of; for if he would have a strong, generous, and pleasant liquor, all further sensible fermentation must be stopt. This is best done by racking off the pure part into open

* If in this state the least hissing noise be heard in the fermenting liquor, the room is too warm; and atmospheric air must be let in at the doors and windows.

vessels, which must be placed in a more cool situation for a day or two:* after which it may again be barrelled and placed in some moderately-cool situation for the winter.† In this situation the cyder will, in course of time, by a sort of insensible fermentation, drop the remainder of its gross lees, become transparent, highly vinous and fragrant. But should the Cyder-maker neglect these precautions, the inevitable consequence will be this—another fermentation will quickly succeed, and convert the fine vinous li-

* The Herefordshire cyder-farmers, after the cyder has perfected its vinous fermentation, place their casks of cyder in open sheds throughout the winter; and when the spring advances, give the last racking, and then cellar it.

† In racking, it is advisable that the stream from the racking-cock be small, and that the receiving-tub be but a small depth below the cock; lest, by exciting a violent motion of the parts of the liquor, another fermentation be brought up. The feculence of the cyder may be strained through a filtering-bag, and placed among the second-rate cyders; but by no means should it be returned to the prime cyder.

B 6

quor he was possessed of into a sort of *vinegar;* and all the art he is master of will never restore it to its former richness and purity.

CHECKING IMPROPER FERMENTATION.

It is possible, however, that a variety of avocations at the season of cyder-making may take off too much of the farmer's attention from this branch of œconomics, and give opportunity to the acetous fermentation to come on ere he is aware of it.—What remedy (it may be asked) has he to prevent the ill effects thereof running to their full extent?—Several have been tried; sometimes with a degree of success, at others wholly unavailable; the most popular ones are the following: A bottle of French brandy; half a gallon of spirit extracted from the lees of cyder, or a pail-full of old cyder, poured into the hogshead, soon after the acetous fermentation is begun: but no wonder if all these should fail, if the cyder be still continued in a close, warm cellar. To give effect to either, it is necessary that the liquor be as much exposed to a cooler air as conveniently may be, and that for a considerable length of time. By such means, it is possible fermentation may, in a great measure, be repressed: and if a cask of *prime* cyder cannot from thence be obtained, a cask of *tolerable*, second-rate cyder may. These remedies are innocent; but if the farmer or Cyder-merchant attempt to cover the accident, occasioned by negligence or inattention, by applying *any preparation of lead*, let him reflect, *that he is about to commit an absolute and unqualified murder on those whose hap it may be to drink his poisonous draught.*

Should, however, any one be wicked enough to sophisticate a cask of cyder with any calxes of lead, his villainy may be detected in the following manner: Make a decoction of orpiment in lime-water, drop a small quantity thereof into a glass of suspected cyder, and if it has been impregnated with any preparation of lead, its colour will soon change to a brown dirty-red, or black; but if it be genuine, its colour will remain nearly the same.—Some liquid liver of sulphur, dropped into a glass of sophistieated cyder, will have a similar effect.—Bishop WATSON directs us to boil together, in a pint of water, an ounce of quick-lime, and half an ounce of flower of brimstone; a few drops of this liquor, being let fall into a glass of cyder containing lead, will change the whole into a colour more or less brown.*

"Calxes of lead," says MACQUER, "having the property of stopping fermentation, might be employed in remedying the acidity of wine, *if lead and all its preparations were not prejudicial to health;* but they occasion

* Chemical Essays, vol. iii. p. 371.

"most terrible cholics, and even DEATH, "when taken internally." The same writer tells us, that even wine may be preserved in the same state by penetrating it with *sulphureous acid*;—from whence we may infer, that the *stumming* a cyder-cask may, at certain seasons, be highly beneficial. *Stumming* is a provincial phrase, signifying the *fuming* a cask with burning sulphur, and is thus performed: Take a strip of canvas cloth, about twelve inches long, and two broad; let it be dipped into melted brimstone. When this match is dry, let it be lighted, and suspended from the bung of a cask (in which there are a few gallons of cyder) until it be burnt out: the cask must remain stopped for an hour or more, and then be rolled to and fro, to incorporate the fumes of the match with the cyder; after which it may be filled. If the stumming be designed only to suppress some slight, improper fermentation, the brimstone match is sufficient; but if it be required to give any additional flavour to the cyder, some powdered ginger, cloves, or cinnamon, &c. may be strewed on the match when it is made;—the burning these ingredients with the sulphur will convey somewhat of their fragrance to the whole cask of cyder; but to do it to the best advantage, it must be performed *as soon* as the vinous fermentation is fully perfected.

FINAL RACKING, ETC.

Let us hope, however, that the Cyderist has succeeded in obtaining a favourable *vinous fermentation*; and that, by a well-timed racking and attention, he has prevented the acetous and other succeeding fermentations from rising; his cyder will then require very little further attention, more than filling up the vessels every two or three weeks, to supply the waste by the insensible fermentation, until the beginning of the next March; at which time it may be reasonably expected he will find his cyder bright and pure, and in a fit state for its final *racking*. This should be done in fair weather; and, if necessary, a commixture should now be made of the high-coloured cyder made from the Jersey, or the luscious sweet apples, with that of the pale-coloured cyder from the poorer sour apples. By which means a general, regular colouring may be obtained with the least trouble, and without expence.

Although it may be expected that the Cyderist will now find his liquor to his mind, both in point of brightness and colour, yet should he be disappointed, the time now is for applying some innocent remedy to remove the disorders.

I shall not recommend to him either of the *forces* commonly used for fining liquors, namely, bullock's-blood, isinglass, eggs, &c. for they as frequently *spoil* a cask of cyder as *improve* it; but if he will put two pounds of lump sugar into a hogshead of cyder, he will receive all the benefit which may be expected from the most nauseous force which nastiness can employ.

If higher colour in cyder be desired than what his fruit naturally gives under the foregoing management, the Cyderist will do well to melt a pound of lump sugar in a stewpan, over a clear fire, stirring it frequently, until it comes to a very dark-brown colour: then to take it off the fire, and as it cools, add some cyder thereto by little and little, and continue stirring it until it becomes a thin uniform fluid. This colouring (about a pint more or less, as occasion may require, to a hogshead) is very cheap and wholesome, tinges to perfection, gives no luscious sweetness, (but rather an agreeable bitterness) and thus recommends itself to the nicer palates.

Soon after this spring racking (and not till then) the casks may be gradually stopped, by first laying the cork on the bung-hole, and in a few days forcing it very tightly into it, covering it over with a layer of melted rosin.

BOTTLING.

In the following month the cyder, in general, will be in a fit state for bottling; but the critical time of this process is when the liquor has acquired in the cask its highest degree of perfection; then, when the weather is fair, the barometer high, and the wind in some northerly point, let the bottles be filled, setting them by uncorked, until the morrow; then let the corks be driven very tightly into the necks of the bottles, tied down with small strong twine or wire, and well secured with melted rosin.

By the month of July following the Cyderist will find himself possessed of a grateful, lively, sparkling, and exhilerating liquor; "highly delicious to the "palate, and congenial to the human "constitution," fit for Princes and the best of their Subjects to regale themselves with.

J. Poole, Printer, Fore-street, Taunton.